GOD .RAGE. ETERNITY

Stephanie Tramaine

God .Rage. Eternity
Copyright © 2017 by Living Word Publishers (His Kingdom Bookshelf)

Edited by Angela Ivey & Living Word Publishers

All rights reserved. No part of this book may be reproduced or transmitted in any form or by any means without written permission from the author.

ISBN 978-0692914236

Printed in USA

Dedication

My heart is filled with so much love for my Lord and Savior Jesus Christ even as I write this dedication. Lord, I want to sincerely thank You for bringing me through every trial and tribulation in my life. I thank You Father, for placing eternity in my heart. You have been my friend, my motivator, my comforter. My desire is to please You and to be with you forever.

To my wonderful parents, Doug and Kathy. I love you guys so very much. I thank God for every sacrifice you have made in order to help me to become successful. You both have been such a pivotal part of my journey and my motivation to aim for the highest. I thank you both for being the best parents you could be and for always encouraging and rooting for me the entire course of my life. I hope I make you both proud.

To my siblings, Doug, Toasha, Terrell, Darian, and Destiny. You all have been such a big part of why I do what I do. We have spent so many years talking about judgment day and what we think will happen. God has showed us so much together and I thank God that my life is tied to each of you. I am so glad that we have journeyed life together and I love you guys endlessly.

To all of my nieces and nephews: Shatina, Doug, Shabriel, Willie, Keith, Artis Jr, Devin, Adrian, Heaven, Makayla, Zachary, Lamarcus, Arianna, Darian Jr, Taiylar, Seon, Seoniyah, Tahj, Zaria and Baby Bell, I love you all and I hope that my life, both the good and the bad is a great example to each of you. I pray for your success often and I believe in each of you. Thank you all for believing in me.

To my support team: Zakayla, Flora, Mavis, Gentile, Mark, Sister Courtney, Herbert and Carolyn Thompson, Pastor and Sister Russell, Alice, Stella, Rashelle, Larry, Emily, Nekole, Tia, Mama Rose, Marunda, Kim, Rozie, Hannah, all of my students and dancers as well as all of my Facebook friends and followers. Thank you so very much for all the love and support you have given me over the years. I love each of you and I thank God for you.

To my Pastors: Tony and Sharlene Barhoo, thank you both for teaching me how to truly have a relationship with the Father. I thank you for all of your prayers, advice, love, support, and patience *you have displayed over the past 11 years. I love you both.*

To Lorraine and Theresa: I miss you so much. I thank you for all the time you both spent encouraging me and helping me. I hope to see you both in heaven.

Acknowledgements

I would like to thank my publisher and friend Veonne Anderson for everything she did for me in the process of creating this book. You pushed me in the right direction.

To LaToya Carey and her husband James for all that you guys did to help me in my photo shoot for this book. God sends the right people at the right time. Thank you for your patience and kindness shown.

To my children Arianna and Devin for being so helpful and supportive during my book writing process. I love you guys so much.

Table of Contents

Dedication	5
Acknowledgements	7
Introduction	17
Chapter 1: Preparation	28
Chapter 2: The Road to Grace	36
Chapter 3: The Issue with the Modern Day Mindset of Society	40
Chapter 4: Professing Christians vs. Authentic Christians	49
Chapter 5: The "Good" Of This World	64
Chapter 6: The Twinkling of an Eye	76
Chapter 7: Hopelessness	82
Chapter 8: outRage	84
Chapter 9: Numbness Following	88
Chapter 10: Amazement in Despair	91
Chapter 11: King of Kings	97
Chapter 12: Life's Story	101
Chapter 13: Obedience > Sacrifice	105
Chapter 14: Lost Souls	109
Chapter 15: Final Destination	112
Chapter 16: The Eternal Abode of Rage...	116
Chapter 17: Angel of Light	120
Chapter 18: Too Late....	124
Chapter 19: Reflection Of Rage	126
Chapter 20: Moving Forward	133
Chapter 21: Relationship with God	165
Chapter 22: Tarry for the Lord	170
Chapter 23: Lord, How Deeply We Need You	185

Chapter 24: Making Jesus our Master and Ruler   202
Chapter 25: God .Rage. Eternity and YOU   210
Chapter 26: Salvation Through Works   216
Chapter 27: Unforgiveness   221
Chapter 28: Rage Was Unrepentant   228
Chapter 29: Rage Walked According to Her Flesh   235
The Horrors of Hell   256

Dear reader,

I want you to know that with the purchase of this book, you have truly gained a sister in Christ. I am dedicated to each of you and would like to become a prayer partner with you.

Please contact me via Facebook at Stephanie Lewis
I am on Instagram at: Onebeautifulstep
Twitter: 1beautifulstep
Please look up my event page on Facebook: Prayerstravaganza

We are live via radio at Word of Praise Radio 91.5FM in the Daytona Beach, FL and Madison, FL area. Please tune in every other Saturday from 1pm-2p (est). We go live via Facebook and you can also tune in at www.wapn.net. You can also call in at (386)673-2495 to share your prayer requests or praise reports. We want to hear from you!! Contact us at www.iamstephanietramaine.com and www.onebeautifulstep.com. You can also email us at thegirlwholovesgod@gmail.com. I am so glad that you are seeking the Lord and I pray that He blesses you abundantly. I will talk with you soon!

Eternally,
Stephanie Tramaine

Preface

So when the apostles were with Jesus, they kept asking him, "Lord, has the time come for you to free Israel and restore our kingdom?" He replied, "The Father alone has the authority to set those dates and times, and they are not for you to know. But you will receive power when the Holy Spirit comes upon you. And you will be my witnesses, telling people about me everywhere—in Jerusalem, throughout Judea, in Samaria, and to the ends of the earth." After saying this, he was taken up into a cloud while they were watching, and they could no longer see him. As they strained to see him rising into heaven, two white-robed men suddenly stood among them. "Men of Galilee," they said, "why are you standing here staring into heaven? Jesus has been taken from you into heaven, but someday he will return from heaven in the same way you saw him go!"

The promises made by Jesus have been fulfilled. Shortly after His ascension, the Holy Spirit came into the hearts of his disciples and followers. This caused the church to grow and testimony of those who were touched by His love to spread His truth. The gospel has been preached across the world. Many people have been saved through faith and the Bible is the best selling in the entire world. Needless to say, the main event that we have been waiting for since the ascension is the promise that the angels made, that He will return just as we saw Him leave...

I was about 7 when God sent me a vision of His return. I had never heard about Jesus coming back, the full truth of the gospel was something I simply didn't know about. In my vision, I woke up to see the clock on my nightstand which was a hand clock spinning around profusely. Scared, I ran out of the room and down the hall to the living room and outside. When I opened the front door, I saw my dad watering the grass. I exclaimed, " Daddy, the time is winding back!" He smiled at me and said, "It's the end of the world baby." Suddenly, I looked up and saw clouds descending from the sky. One the clouds were angels dressed in white. I also saw Jesus. They landed right in my front yard. There were people gathering and the ground opened up. Those who were wrapped up almost like mummies were thrown into the fire which was in the hole. I was very frightened and stepped back. I started thinking of how I didn't want to end up there. In an instant, I was on a cloud, ready to return with Jesus. My concern then became whether my daddy would make it in. I looked on the cloud to my right and I saw him standing there in his painting clothes, smiling and waving. When I had this dream and told my father, he was surprised due to the fact that he had never told me about the rapture or judgment day. He knew that it had to be a vision sent by God to show me my destiny. Since then, my heart has been tuned into things eternal. My heart's desire is to help others to be tuned into the same thing, to help them to plan out and live out their lives with their eternal destination in mind. It is so imperative to me to let others know about the love of God, and the dangers of not being prepared when the time comes. Every part of me desires each person I have ever encountered to make it in. Deep inside, I yearn to tell everyone everywhere to be prepared. It would break my heart to see anyone not make in. This is what drives me to tell as many as will listen what the Word of God says about what is to come.

Introduction

Eternity. It is definitely something that most people do not think of everyday. Some even choose not to believe in its existence. I believe it is because everything we do is measured in time. We use it to decide when to wake up, when to go to sleep, when to arrive to work or school, and even determine when it is appropriate to have the privilege of drinking or driving based on it. We try our best to manage our time well, but often it passes without us even noticing. Women get anxious if too much time has passed if they haven't reproduced or gotten married. People who are incarcerated sometimes obsess over time, as the passage a particular amount of time determines their freedom. Time is the currency of life. If spent well, one can live richly, enjoying the passage of it without regret. However, if spent unwisely, one can live his or her latter days wallowing in despair. I can personally say that I have both made the most of my time as well as had years of time that I honestly felt was completely wasted. Although I wish with everything that I am that I could get that time back or at least make up for it, the only thing that I can really do is reflect on it and place even more value on the time I have left. Time is a strange thing, as it is something treasured when it passes, and many wish to be able to get it back once it is gone away. I remember in my teen years, I wished it would hurry up and pass quickly so that I could make my own choices as an adult. As an adult, I have often wished that I could go back and redo my time spent as an adolescent. Time can sometimes be spent frivolously on our lazy days. I have see days go by with me just watching television or surfing the web. The time passes by so quickly it makes me wish I had better spent it. One thing we can all agree on is that once it is gone, there is nothing we can do to bring it back.

  This reality is not something that everyone can grasp. In recent years, I have heard many people state "YOLO" (You only live once). The theology of this phrase leads followers to make dangerous choices, not based on well thought out consideration on the consequences of the said choice. Many believe that they can let all inhibitions go and just do what they feel because, well, you only live once. While I understand that this is something unbelievers may embrace as truth, believers should not entertain it. The thought that one only has this life to live and that the choices therein should be based on how much fun the experience is, rather than the weight of the repercussions is foolishness. As a believer, we should strive to make each choice based on the determination of whether the choice lines up with the life of Christ. He is our example of how to live. So what does the bible say about the term YOLO? I know one would think that such terms are new in nature and that the bible is ancient. Therefore it could not possibly hold the answer to whether using such new millennial terminology is detrimental to a believer. Au contraire mon frère. God's word reveals the truth in various scripture.

Digging into my favorite book, Ecclesiastes, Paul tells us that

'What has been will be again, what has been done will be done again; there is nothing new under the sun' (Ecclesiastes 1:9).

Surely many people have heard this truth, and dismissed it as a cliché phrase. But evidence surrounding the concept of YOLO is no different. In 1 Corinthians 15:32 Paul spoke about such hopelessness about eternity by stating **"Let us eat and drink, for tomorrow we die."** This was a declaration in reference to those who did not believe in the power of the resurrection of Christ, which in itself promises us eternity with Him if we obey His commandments. To think of life as something that we only have to live once is deceptive in itself. The further deception that during our lives, we have to grasp the opportunities as they come, thinking about their consequences or responsibilities they bring later, is not of God. In doing so, we are much like the people who didn't believe in the resurrection of Jesus Christ. This may not affect a non believer, but if you are a believer who has at any time lived your life according to the concept of YOLO, it should send a sobering reality to your heart.

Or maybe it doesn't. It is evident that not all Christians believe in heaven and hell. This is absurd, it seems pretty irrational to me. Merriam-Webster defines Christians as : **one who professes belief in the teachings of Jesus Christ.** This is pretty self explanatory in truth, if we claim Christianity, we are professing belief in God's Word. Christ taught old and new testament as well, so that puts to rest any debate on which of the Testaments we as Christians follow. If we look into our bible, Jesus often spoke of hell. Matthew Slick of Christian Apologetics & Research Ministry estimated that in the Bible there are anywhere from 13 to 23 times that the word "hell" is referenced. Many of the references to hell are made by Jesus Christ. Here are a few examples of direct quotes from Jesus Himself:

Matthew 5:22, "But I say to you that everyone who is angry with his brother will be liable to judgment; whoever insults his brother will be liable to the council; and whoever says, 'You fool!' will be liable to the

hell fire."

Matt. 5:29, "If your right eye causes you to sin, tear it out and throw it away. For it is better that you lose one of your members than that your whole body be thrown into hell."

Matt. 5:30, "And if your right hand causes you to sin, cut it off and throw it away. For it is better that you lose one of your members than that your whole body go into hell."

Matt. 10:28, "And do not fear those who kill the body but cannot kill the soul. Rather fear him who can destroy both soul and body in hell."

Matt. 18:9, "And if your eye causes you to sin, tear it out and throw it away. It is better for you to enter life with one eye than with two eyes to be thrown into the hell of fire."

Matt. 23:15, "Woe to you, scribes and Pharisees, hypocrites! For you travel across sea and land to make a single proselyte, and when he becomes a proselyte, you make him twice as much a child of hell as yourselves."

Matt. 23:33, "You serpents, you brood of vipers, how are you to escape being sentenced to hell?"

Now if Christians profess to believe in Jesus Christ, and He spoke of hell as often as He did, why is it that not all of them actually believe that hell exists? Is it because somehow we have mixed doctrine of the world with the doctrine of the Holy Bible? Is it because it feels better to believe that anyone who believes in Christ will get a free pass to heaven? Perhaps. In truth, no matter the reasons for the discord among the believers, it reveals a great fallacy that needs to be addressed. I believe that if you were to hear about a harmful disease that is hospitalizing or even worse killing people, you would instantly tune into details of the disease. Why? Because you want to prevent yourself from contracting it. So you watch the news, find out all you need to know so you and your family is safe. Some would even go as far to finding out statistical data of where it has struck in the area, and warn their children, friends and extended family about the risks of contracting the said disease. Surely one would not want any of his/her loved ones to risk being exposed to anything of that sort. Belief in hell in itself, in the same way, opens up the questions of what it is, where it is, why do people go there, and my favorite, *'how do I prevent myself from being there?'*

A few years back, I was watching a movie about heaven. I was shocked at the fact that one of the main characters, who was a Pastor, questioned the existence of heaven. I remember thinking, "How can he be preaching and professing the gospel when he didn't know whether he believed in what he preached?" In my small world everyone I knew to be a believer knew and understood the truth about Heaven's existence as well as hell. It is something that is so commonly preached, and I know personally that it is something that I consider daily. I think about questions like, 'Where will I be when the rapture happens? What will transpire when I stand before Jesus? Will I have done enough? Am I ready today?' Due to the fact that I think about it so often, I felt that those around me, especially in the Christian community, would be thinking about it as well. However, after gaining a pretty sizable Facebook following, I realized it was not as common to think about as I had previously supposed. Many times when I refer to the afterlife or eternity, people will flood my inbox asking questions about what they need to do to be prepared. Some even begin to dig deeper into what sins they are guilty of and ask for prayer so that they can gain the strength to walk away before it's too late. Please understand dear reader, that it is never too late. God's mercy is renewed every morning. No matter what sin you have committed, Our Father in Heaven is faithful to forgive. He is able! I pray that you are moved to seek God even right now so that your name will be found in the book of life!

My favorite conversations about eternity are to little children. They are fascinated with how this world will one day be a memory and that there is a new life they will experience either with Jesus or apart from Him based on their choices. Sometimes in Children's Church, they go over the allotted amount of time for service, raising their hands and trying to discover more about eternity. The bible verse that comes to mind is Matthew 9:37 which states, **"the harvest is plentiful, but the laborers are few."** The children as well as my Facebook followers are all hungry to know more about eternity and what awaits them. Once it is brought up, they seek earnestly for answers on the how and the why behind salvation and it drives many to self-exploration of what they can do to be saved. How about you? Are you curious about the afterlife? Do you believe in it? Are you living in a way that would place you on the right side of eternity? It is a subject that i believe is so important to share as often as possible because God's Word warns us in Deuteronomy 6:4-9:

Love the Lord your God with all your heart and with all your soul and with all your strength. These commandments that I give you today are to be on your hearts. Impress them on your children. Talk about them when you sit at home and when you walk along the road, when you lie down and when you get up. Tie them as symbols on your hands and bind them on your foreheads. Write them on the doorframes of your houses and on your gates.

On the contrary, many times, we get so caught up in just teaching the bible stories or just quoting well known scriptures that we overlook the need to prepare for the future that is to come as it is written in the book of Revelations. I truly believe that if we continue to teach our children, family and friends on the subject of eternity, and exhort them to really examine their walk continuously, it will prevent great despair on judgment day. Jesus Himself speaks about that day and describes in Matthew 7:22

"On judgment day many will say to me, 'Lord! Lord! We prophesied in your name and cast out demons in your name and performed many miracles in your name. But I will reply, 'I

never knew you. Get away from me, you who break God's laws.'

Can you imagine how horrible it would feel to be turned away from Jesus on the last day? I mean, even when I was unsaved, this was something that I feared. Who wants to be turned away? However, in order to be assured that we will indeed make it into heaven, we have to be prepared to go. This is a sad truth that should drive the believer and unbeliever alike, right to the feet of Jesus to examine their hearts and motives and see what must they do to be ready for that great and sure day.

Chapter 1: Preparation

So the obvious question becomes are you ready? Have you diligently looked over your life and the choices that you have made? Have you determined that everything is in order? I want you to really take a moment and look over every detail of your life. Can you say that you are following the Lord completely? Is there a problem that you just can't seem to gain control over? The time to be honest is now. The bible tells us in 1 Corinthians 15:52 that

In a moment, in a twinkling of an eye that the trumpet will sound.

Think about this for a moment or two. I used to think that if you blink your eyes, that is how quickly the moment will come. I recently came to understand that a twinkling of the eye is even quicker than the blink of an eye. The twinkling of an eye is amazingly fast. In the article called "Thoughts from Timothy" Doug Forkner writes,

"Scientists tell us that we have a wink, and blink, and a twink. The twink is the amount of time that it takes light to enter the eye, reflect off the retina and be seen. With light traveling at

386,000 miles per hour, that means a twinkle is around 1/6 billionth of a second. That's fast! In other words, you will not have time to make things right with the Lord when He comes! One moment we will be here...and the next moment we will be with Him!"

This article blew my mind! How quickly the rapture will happen! In that small time, there is no time for repentance, reflection or correction. In the twinkling of an eye, there is no time to call loved ones to see if they are in a place of preparation. The bible paints an even scarier picture. In Matthew 24:36-44, Jesus Himself states:

But of that day and hour no one knows, not even the angels of heaven, but My Father only. But as the days of Noah were, so also will the coming of the Son of Man be. For as in the days before the flood, they were eating and drinking, marrying and giving in marriage, until the day that Noah entered the ark, and did not know until the flood came and took them all away, so also will the coming of the Son of Man be. Then two men will be in the field: one will be taken and the other left. Two women will be grinding at the mill: one will be taken and the other left. Watch therefore, for you do not know what hour your Lord is coming. But know this, that if the master of the house had known what hour the

thief would come, he would have watched and not allowed his house to be broken into. Therefore you also be ready, for the Son of Man is coming at an hour you do not expect.

Jesus was saying so much in this scripture. The reading of the fact that two people who are together in one place will be separated makes me very cautious. Can you imagine your husband, your wife, parent, best friend, or child being one and you being the other? In less than a second, you could be separated from them forever. My heart yearns for God just at that thought. Dear reader, we have to get this thing right. The time is truly now for salvation!

The problem lies within the reasoning behind many people on why they believe they are in a place of security with the Lord. Maybe you have been led to believe the tale of "God knows my heart." This phrase has been so familiar to me throughout my life. This belief system is based on God's sovereignty. People who follow this ideology understand that God is a loving God. They believe that He knows all, and may truly conclude that because they want to do well, but sometimes make mistakes, God will see past their mistakes and judge them based on their heart's desire to do what He says they should do. This falsehood is so dangerous, and I want to clarify that through the word.

Jeremiah 17:9
The heart is deceitful above all things, and desperately wicked: who can know it?

Romans 6:1-4
What shall we say then? Shall we continue in sin, that grace may abound? God forbid. How shall we, that are dead to sin, live any longer therein? Know ye not, that so many of us as were baptized into Jesus Christ were baptized into his death? Therefore we are buried with him by baptism into death: that like as Christ was raised up from the dead by the glory of the Father, even so we also should walk in newness of life.

Paul is exhorting the Romans to live for Christ, which means embracing grace by letting go of sin. To believe that you can continue in sin and be forgiven based on the fact that you want to do well nullifies the sacrifice Jesus made on the cross. If all it takes for salvation is to have a heart that yearns to do right, then Jesus would not have had to die on the cross. Our bible tells us that the wages of sin is death. Christ's ultimate sacrifice is what saves us. The Holy Spirit is what helps us to live a life that is pleasing and to produce the obedience that we yearn to have.

For me, it took at least 30 years of my life to realize this concept. Not that I had not been in church all my life. My father is a minister of music. I have traveled with him to his many churches and learned the word as long as I can remember. However, I had also been given the example that good people sometimes do bad, and that God sees their hearts, understands their mistakes and will accept them as they are. I felt safe in allowing some sin into my life. I honestly believed that I was good with God as long as it wasn't serious sins, like sexual immorality (not to say i didn't engage in that for many years), or as long as I didn't commit murder, or some "big sin" that was frowned upon with believers. I believed that it also didn't matter how I treated people, as long as in my heart I believed in Jesus Christ and that I tried when possible to get along with people. These were truths that were not biblically correct, but traditionally in my family and among peers were accepted as fact. This is where it can become very dangerous for a believer. We begin practicing false teaching that is not based on God's Word or even remotely close to anything that He has stated in scriptures. Then we pass it down to our children and accept it in peer circles and sure enough we are all led into lukewarmness. This category of sin is not something that most people consider themselves as being in. Nonetheless, when we accept any form of sin, that is exactly what we are doing. I am telling you what I know. Not because someone has told me but because of what I lived. It wasn't until I was a member of a bible-believing ministry that taught truth and encouraged me to search the scriptures for myself that I was able to see the error in my way. God requires complete obedience, plain and simple. What does all of this have to do with YOLO, or believing that God's sovereign knowledge of your heart's intentions? Everything.

If we as believers don't earnestly seek God and ask Him for grace to live by His word and do His will then we will find ourselves locked out of the kingdom. I have seen and heard people say that heaven is a place that everyone will go to, in spite of their belief systems and religious practices. This can be no further from the truth. Even believers practicing in the churches in the highest of leadership positions are at risk of the hellfire. I am not giving you my opinion, but telling you what is in the Word of God. Let me again rephrase to you that in Matthew 7:22, Jesus said that on the day of judgment,

'Many will say to me on that day, 'Lord, Lord, did we not prophesy in your name and in your name drive out demons and in your name perform many miracles? Then I will

tell them plainly, 'I never knew you. Away from me, you evildoers!'

Follow me now, this was Jesus saying these words to believers. These weren't people who chose to follow Buddha or Hinduism or Islam. These were people who believed in Jesus and even were inside the church performing miracles. They were driving out demons...they even stated that it was in Jesus's name! But for some reason they had come up short and were turned away from Jesus in the day of Judgment. I want you to understand these words and let them marinate in your heart.

Chapter 2: The Road to Grace

So now you may be asking well what is grace? Merriam-Webster's definition describes grace as **unmerited divine assistance given humans for their regeneration or sanctification.** God gives us unmerited divine assistance to do HIS WILL and obey His commands. This is through the Holy Spirit, which is a gift given to us when we receive Jesus Christ as our Lord and Savior and are baptized with the Holy Spirit. To better understand how grace works, here is a scenario to make it plain. Imagine, if you will, that you are on a boat that is sinking. The only way to avoid death would be to get to an island, which is a day's journey by boat away. You know that there is no way to get to the island without a boat because the journey is entirely too long to swim. Sadly, you try to prepare mentally for death, which is your fate whether you try to swim, or not. Amazingly, someone comes along and informs you that they have access to a boat that is brand new and is fully stocked with food and supplies for the journey. All you have to do is get on the boat. Grace is that boat full of supplies and Jesus would be the person who gave you the boat. What would your response be? Living a life with the mindset of 'God knows my heart' would be equivalent to you saying, "I have the boat and God knows I want to get to the island, but I am not going to get on it and go." However, if you want to save your life, then the only logical action would be to get on the boat and go to safety. The same practical common sense action would be applied to your spiritual life. Saying 'God knows my heart' is not enough. God has not asked you to only have great intentions. God is asking you to obey Him. Jesus says, "If you love me, keep my commandments." Jesus desires us to place actions that coincide with our intentions. I want you to think about being employed. When you get hired for a company they usually give you an employee handbook that outlines their rules and expectations from you. Upon being hired if you tell them, "You know my heart, I want to be a good employee." However, you are never to work on time, many times calling in when you have a shift or committing what employers call a 'no call, no show'. You are stealing money and sleeping on the job. What do you think your employer would do? I believe that they would probably review with you the rules and policies and judge you on whether your actions line up with their expectations. Obviously, because you are committing numerous infractions consistently, they would have to let you go. I must say this would in all means be absolutely fair. Your employers hired you with expectation that you would follow their handbook and do what they required. How much more has God called you to fulfill what He has created you to do and to obey Him? Grace requires consistent actions geared toward fulfilling God's will for your life. Following God's commandments is a vital part of being His follower.

    Upon realizing that my walk with Christ is revealed not only intentions, but also actions, I was shocked. In truth, if anyone really does believe that God's Word is true, then they should live by it. Everything you do should be based on the fact that you believe God said what He said so you should do what He says. What my sinful heart began to acknowledge was that I had been blind to God's Word. This was a scary revelation and one I hated to accept but I couldn't escape the truth. I begin to see first and foremost that I was not very different from unbelievers, even though I regularly attended church and prayed and sometimes read my bible. It started becoming quite clear to me that my belief in Christ and that He died for my sins wasn't enough to separate me from the very sins that He died for. This sobering reality didn't come with just one or two days of attending church or bible study. It didn't hit me all at once, though it would be nice to say that it did. In contradiction, I lived many years of my life as a Christian regularly attending church, teaching

Sunday School, children's church, attending ministry courses and being a leader in the Christian church, still very much in sin. I didn't understand the truth in the fact that whom the Son sets free is free indeed. Perhaps you are reading this and thinking that all of this applies to you in some way, if so I promise you that this book is going to change the way you think about sin, time, and eternity.

Please pray with me:

Most Gracious and Heavenly Father, I come to you humbly and ask You to bless me, your child. I pray that You will allow the Spirit of the Living God to fill my heart and to open my spiritual eyes and heart as I read this book. I come into agreement with Stephanie that I will be able to understand the Truth of Your Word. I pray that the urgency of preparation for my eternal home will fill my spirit. I also ask You Lord, to help me to become a voice in these last and evil days to proclaim the truth of Your Word to your people. I pray all of this in Jesus name, Amen.

Chapter 3: The Issue with the Modern Day Mindset of Society

Think about it. From the time we are born, we are full of selfish desires. If you are a parent or have ever been in the vicinity of a newborn child, you know that the average infant cries very often. It doesn't matter if you are trying to sleep or if you are in a quiet church service. Even if you aren't feeling well, or if you are on the phone, they cry all the time with no regard to your feelings. I have 17 nieces and nephews. Babysitting them as newborns was one of the hardest things to do. One of my nephews had colic and he would cry even more than the average child. Sometimes even holding and rocking him when he was upset didn't stop the crying. I quickly realized that it didn't matter what I was doing when he would start the crying. He was in no way concerned about how his outbursts of crying affected me. The only thing he was concerned about is his needs or desires to be held, changed, fed and/or burped. This pretty much holds true throughout the newborn stages. As the child grows into toddler years, one can expect to have many of our household items and/or jewelry broken or misplaced by the toddler who is unaware of their value and unable to see past their desire to play with glass items or take jewelry and flush it down the toilet. One of my nieces loved her pacifier more than anything. She affectionately called it her "pap pap". Well, many times the pacifier would go missing. She would cry and cry until we replaced it with a similar one. This would happen more and more often. My sister would get very upset with me as I was often with her when it would go missing. She and I would search for them all of the time, to no avail. It was as if they had vanished into thin air. Of course, asking my niece if she knew where the pacifier was didn't produce any results. She would just cry even more. My sister was forced to go and buy more for her. It was quite frustrating. Finally one day, she walked into the kitchen. Curious to know what she was doing (she was 1-2 at the time), I followed her into the kitchen. Not noticing me behind her, she ran to the refrigerator and threw the pacifier in the space next to the fridge. I was shocked. When we pulled the refrigerator back, we realized where the pacifiers had "disappeared" to. I still remind her of this story today. Her little game of hiding the pacifier had caused us much grief, but at the time it didn't matter to her. She was just fascinated with throwing the pacifier. Moving into the preschool years, you can look forward to temper tantrums when he/she doesn't get what they want. My other niece was the princess of temper tantrums. She would get into a public place and cry and scream until she got what she wanted. This was quite embarrassing, as you never knew when she should fall out or scream. Perhaps you know some kids that are this way. Not to say that children do this on purpose. They have to eventually be taught that other people have needs and that they are to control their emotions. The beautiful job of parenting can transform that selfish toddler into an individual that is empathetic, caring and responsible. However, it doesn't necessarily eliminate the selfishness that is held in the hearts of society.

    This is true because society is bred on selfishness. Even as children we are taught to pursue our desires and our dreams. I remember being as young as 7 or 8 and being told to start thinking about my future and what it was that I wanted to pursue as a career. I would often think of being a teacher. I would fantasize about being in a classroom full of children and being able to teach them the same things that I loved about school. My heart was set on being the best teacher that I could be. Then as I got older, I realized that certain careers held the potential to make more money. I ended up looking into more prestigious careers like being a lawyer. When I was in 8th grade, I found out that the high school that was recently built had an academy for law and government. I was absolutely excited!! Not only would I be able to go to a prestigious academy, but it had the added perks of going to school with my middle school sweetheart. I begged and begged my mother to sign the paperwork for the school. She was hesitant because it was so far away. "But it's the academy for law, and I want to be a lawyer," I told her. I left out the fact that my motivation was laced in selfishness of seeking to be with my boyfriend as well. She eventually signed and I got into the school. Being that it was the only school at the time that had such a program, many of my classmates were children of judges, lawyers and other prestigious careers. Prior to my high school years, I had been surrounded with people who for the most part, had the same income as my parents (maybe a little more but not much). Now I was in school with teens who had brand new cars by 10th grade. We talked often about the perks of having money and how much income could be made by lawyers. We even had the opportunity to meet with actual lawyers and judges and learn about how much they made as part of our curriculum. This slapped away any goals of me becoming a teacher. Why be a teacher when there was so much money to be made in the field of law? My goals became based primarily on how much money I stood to make, rather than something that I desired to actually do. Society would praise me for either even though both ways of thinking were in complete error. Of course, much of society doesn't recognize it as such. To be driven by the success that this world has to offer is something that is highly esteemed in this world. However the bible warns us in Luke 16:15 of the danger in that...

Then he said to them, "You like to appear righteous in public, but God knows your hearts. What is highly esteemed by man is detestable in the sight of God."

The definition of detestable in Merriam-Webster is **arousing or meriting intense dislike**. Jesus is saying that wanting those things that society esteems deserves an intense dislike in His eyes. The synonyms for this word stood out even more. They are as follows:

Abhorrent, hateful, loathsome, despicable, abominable, execrable, repellant, repugnant, repulsive, revolting, disgusting, distasteful, horrible, horrid, awful.

I feel like being involved with anything that makes the Lord feel that way is unwise to say the least. Can you imagine being in a relationship with someone, and you tell them "Honey, I don't like when you do _____ because it is abominable, disgusting, and (all of the words that are synonyms to detestable) my sight." The person who is in the relationship with you should easily agree not to do that particular action if they truly love you. Why do we feel we have the right to commit these actions in spite of how God feels? Then to add insult to injury, we will in the same breath proclaim our love for Him. How? How is it that we can say with assurance, "I love God" when we are busy chasing those detestable things God hates? This really is something that we need to think about and seek to change if we really love God. Now being in the academy wasn't a bad thing, there was no evil in that. Being driven by the things that are highly esteemed by man was where my error lied. God desires His children to seek treasures in heaven, not on earth. This is for many reasons, but one of the main ones that I have discovered is that He created us with a purpose to fulfill. That purpose was something that was not going to be fulfilled if all I was concerned about was my own desires. I could've easily been fooled into continuing in my own selfishness of seeking out the things that I wanted. It would have been easy to never pay any attention to God outside of making sure I told Him more of what I wanted. My life could've been centered around asking Him to bless me in that selfishness. However, that would have left me in a place where I would have never truly known God. Yes, because I came from a family of believers and truly loved to go to church and to profess the gospel of Christ, I would have always been in somebody's congregation. That doesn't necessarily mean that I would end up hearing "well done, thy good and thy faithful servant." These are the words that the majority of believers know God will say to them (or at least hope that God will say to them) at the time of judgment. Nonetheless, if I have not been faithful in any way, always seeking my own desires and never fully committing my entire life to the will of God, then there was truly no way that I could ever expect to hear those words in reality. Nothing was "well" or "good" about my own self-gratifying ways. How could I possibly believe that anything I did made me heaven ready? I was living in true deception. This was a hard pill to swallow because we as Christians believe that we are different. We fall into the trap of looking around us at people who are engulfed in sin and say, "Well, I don't do this, or I have never done that," and deem ourselves as in right standing with God. Just because we aren't as "bad" as non-believers, doesn't place us in right standing with God. I was truly deceived to believe my simple profession of the gospel made me a Christian. The truth was that I was far from being authentic.

Chapter 4: Professing Christians vs. Authentic Christians

Let me repeat that I was a Christian. I believed that Jesus was the Son of God. I believed in the trinity and that God was somewhere watching over me. I would memorize and quote scriptures, and use His word to encourage others. I would often pray and ask God to bless me in everything I do. All of these were good things, indeed. None of them were able to save me from a burning hell. When we search the Word of God, it is clear that belief in God's existence is not enough. However, many people believe this is their saving grace. Beloved this is a grave error. To top it off, we have many churches with more faith in the sinner's prayer than the power of the Holy Spirit. Somehow, people believe that if they recite the prayer, then they have a free pass to salvation and deliverance from hell. There is so much inaccuracy in this assumption and approach to heaven. To be motivated to come to Jesus based on the fear of being doomed to hell is not a pure rationale. Yet churches everywhere will view the sinner who comes to seek salvation based solely on fear of eternal damnation as being sagacious. These individuals, who have not truly sought out God for the remission of their sins nor came to the point of true repentance, have no move of the Holy Spirit. Therefore, they are leaving the altar as much of a sinner as they were when they came. Sadly, many live out their entire life with the falsehood of sinners prayer security. God have mercy. Without true repentance, there is no salvation. It is written In Romans 10:2-4 :

For I bear them witness that they have a zeal for God, but not according to knowledge. For they being ignorant of God's righteousness, and seeking to establish their own righteousness, have not submitted to the righteousness of God. For Christ is the end of the law for righteousness to everyone who believes.

There are so many people who are foolishly relying on sinners' prayers that were made many years ago. Sad to say, this is not enough. We need to experience a true relationship with God that involves so very much. To think that the prayer recited is enough for God to welcome you into heaven with open arms is completely wrong. To think that sitting in the church and saying "Amen" and "Thank you Jesus" is going to make you heaven bound very wrong. An old saying is "Sitting in the church doesn't make you a Christian any more than sitting in the garage makes you a car." Your faith has to be accompanied with a relationship with God. Your belief in the existence of God is not equivalent to a relationship with Him. The bible tells us in James 2:19,

You say you have faith, for you believe that there is one God. Good for you! Even the demons believe this, and they tremble in terror.

This verse is very powerful. It clearly shows us that faith in God is something even demons have. If it were in fact true that the belief in His existence was enough, then even the demons would be 'saved'. For a long time I was a professing Christian. I thought that if I just in my heart 'believed' in Jesus Christ and professed it to other people, as well as went to church, and read my bible every now and then I was set. How wrong was I!

The professing Christian is misguided in every way. In spite of the proclamations and false assumption of being saved and delivered, the truth is that one never really is 100% sure of their salvation. I remember when I was living as a professing Christian, I would say the sinner's prayer every time I heard it. I was convinced each time that the Pastor called for those who didn't know the Lord Jesus

Christ as their savior to come forth, I needed to be there. Time and time again I would go to the altar and cry out to God, asking Him over and over again to save and deliver me from my sins. I would leave the altar, sure of my salvation for only a short amount of time. Then the next time that I had the opportunity, I would go up to the altar again, asking for the same blessing. If I were reading Christian material, I would come across the sinner's prayer and pray it again. This cycle became a normal routine and I could easily say I have recited it maybe hundreds of time. It seemed that no matter what I did, no matter how many times I had recited the prayer and invited Jesus into my heart, at the end of the day, I was not sure in my salvation. Perhaps you have felt the same way at one time or another. You read the prayer again and again, yet salvation is never really settled in your heart. This reminds me of what was said to the woman at the well by Jesus Himself.

John 4:13-14
Jesus answered and said to her, "Whoever drinks of this water will thirst again, but whoever drinks of the water that I shall give him will never thirst. But the water that I shall give him will become in him a fountain of water springing up into everlasting life."

Jesus spoke to this woman about the Holy Spirit. He is the water that fills you up to where you will never thirst again. When I was professing God without the power and presence of the Holy Spirit, I was operating on my own faith. I would make up my mind to stop sinning, and do it over and over again. Due to the fact that I was simply a professing Christian and not an authentic Christian, I was missing a key element in being able to truly receive salvation. I needed the Holy Spirit. He was the only being that would be able to help me to just stop it with all of the professing and really be about my Father's business. He is the One to help me to be able to face my own selfish nature and become transformed to the mind of Christ. Without Him, I was no better than the demons who tremble at the name of Jesus. I definitely needed Him. Once you receive the Holy Spirit, you become a new creature. This is what the bible means to be born again. No longer will you be a self-seeking, self-serving individual, but you will be made whole in Jesus Christ. No longer will your desire be the things of this world. You will be made new. You mind, your heart will seek the things of Jesus Christ. Beloved, if you are a believer, it is so important for you to be able to examine your heart, your motives, your intent. If it is not centered around the kingdom of heaven and winning souls for Christ, you may need to ask the

Father for the gift of the Holy Spirit. Without Him, we will fall into the mindset of the world , forever seeking the things in it. In the days of Jesus, there was a ruler named Nicodemus who came to Him, seeking for answers to being able to inherit eternal life. Here is how it went:

There was a man of the Pharisees named Nicodemus, a ruler of the Jews. This man came to Jesus by night and said to Him, "Rabbi, we know that You are a teacher come from God; for no one can do these signs that You do unless God is with him." Jesus answered and said to him, "Most assuredly, I say to you, unless one is born again, he cannot see the kingdom of God." Nicodemus said to Him, "How can a man be born when he is old? Can he enter a second time into his mother's womb and be born?" Jesus answered, "Most assuredly, I say to you, unless one is born of water and the Spirit, he cannot enter the kingdom of God. That which is born of the flesh is flesh, and that which is born of the Spirit is spirit. Do not marvel that I said to you, 'You must be born again.' The wind blows where it wishes, and you hear the sound of it, but cannot tell where it comes from and where it goes. So is everyone who is born of the Spirit." Nicodemus answered and said to Him, "How can these things be?" Jesus answered and said to him, "Are you the teacher of Israel, and do not *know these things? Most assuredly, I say to you, We speak what We know and testify what We have seen, and you do not receive Our witness. If I have told you earthly things and you do not believe, how will you believe if I tell you heavenly things? No one has ascended to heaven but He who came down from heaven, that is, the Son of Man who is in heaven. And as Moses lifted up the serpent in the wilderness, even so must the Son of Man be lifted up, that whoever believes in Him should not perish but have eternal life. <u>For God so loved the world that He gave His only begotten Son, that whoever believes in Him should not perish but have everlasting life.</u> For God did not send His Son into the world to condemn the world, but that the world through Him might be saved. "He who believes in Him is not condemned; but he who does not believe is condemned already, because he has not believed in the name of the only begotten Son of God. And this is the condemnation, that the light has come into the world, and men loved darkness rather than light, because their deeds were evil. For everyone practicing evil hates the light and does not come to the light, lest his deeds should be exposed. But he who does the truth comes to the light, that his deeds may be clearly seen, that they have been done in God."*

There is much to be said in these verses, but you can see that there is an action that needs to take place. Professing believers can profess all day, attending many church services and offering money to the poor as well, but outside of being born again, they will always be without assurance in their salvation. Jesus didn't tell Nicodemus that he had to give a certain amount of money, or attend a prestigious school of ministry, or get license to minister. He told him that whosoever believed in Him should not perish, but have everlasting life. You may be thinking, "well professing Christians do believe in Him." However, in this case The Greek word for believe (pisteuo) has a deeper meaning than simply agreeing with the facts; it means personal commitment. Moreover, in the original language of the New Testament, "believe" means a personal commitment to Jesus Christ, not a simple intellectual agreement. When you are able to gain the Holy Spirit, it is a relationship with Jesus Christ. You move from just professing your belief in Him to committing to Him. It would be just as if you meet someone who you think is attractive. You may say, he/she is someone who you are interested in, that you like what they look like, what they say, the way they dress. However, until you really are able to commit to that person, you aren't in a relationship. Therefore, you may have other people that catch your eye, you may go through phases where you are even dating other people. In the same sense, without commitment to Christ, one is left seeking things of God mingled with the things of the world, and left wanting because no true commitment has been made. I have personally met many people outside of the church who have made comments about professed believers who commit sin and act worse than some people outside of the church. They say things like "That's why I don't go to church, all of the people in the church sin worse than people outside of the church." This is because of the commitment that has been lacking in that church goers life. I was married for 7 years and ended up divorced. After I had been single for some time, I ended up on the dating scene again. So much had changed. I felt old and left behind on the "new" standards of dating. When I had dated before, people would meet each other, go on a few dates, talk on the phone, and then get into a committed relationship. It was simple. Not so with the "new" way of dating. People would meet you, like you, tell you of how special you are to them, spend everyday with you, and never commit to you. That way, if you were to ever question them about someone else that they are possibly dating, they would tell you that you're not in a relationship. I would wonder why would you spend so much time and energy with a person and never commit? Well, it was because that individual may have genuinely had an interest in you, but did not want to let go of prospective mates that may come along. Looking back, it mirrors the hearts of those uncommitted to God. They love His ways, they want to reap every benefit that God has to offer, but they don't love Him enough to let go of everything else and truly commit to Him. I know that I didn't like this "new" way of dating or how it made me feel less than worthy of a relationship. How do you imagine this type of relationship makes God feel? Their errors only push others away from the church and God. If you are a true and authentic Christian, it will be an easy decision to turn from everything else and choose God. The bible tells us in Matthew 13:44-50

"Again, the kingdom of heaven is like treasure hidden in a field, which a man found and hid; and for joy over it he goes and sells all that he has and buys that field. "Again, the kingdom of heaven is like a merchant seeking beautiful pearls, who, when he had found one pearl of great price, went and sold all that he had and bought it. "Again, the kingdom of heaven is like a dragnet that was cast into the sea and gathered some of every kind, which, when it

was full, they drew to shore; and they sat down and gathered the good into vessels, but threw the bad away. So it will be at the end of the age. The angels will come forth, separate the wicked from among the just, and cast them into the furnace of fire. There will be wailing and gnashing of teeth."

The professing Christian never really does choose God wholeheartedly. Therefore without true repentance, they will be considered just as the wicked. The furnace of fire is all they have to look forward to, because they valued the things of the world over the things of God. You have to let one go.

The Authentic Believer

The authentic believer has made the commitment to God. He/she is constantly seeking the will of God for their lives and living to fulfill it. The authentic believer is someone who is committed to God in every way, and doesn't mind Him stepping in his/her life and recalibrating and recalculating their destination, for the authentic believer knows that what God has for them is far greater than anything that the world has to offer. The authentic believer is also able to endure trials and tribulations, knowing that God is there, and is able to trust the truth of His

Word. This is so important because the bible reveals that trials will come. In 1 Peter 4, the bible states,

1 Peter 4:12-14

Beloved, do not think it strange concerning the fiery trial which is to try you, as though some strange thing happened to you; but rejoice to the extent that you partake of Christ's sufferings, that when His glory is revealed, you may also be glad with exceeding joy. If you are reproached for the name of Christ, blessed are you, for the Spirit of glory and of God rests upon you. On their part He is blasphemed, but on your part He is glorified.

As I stated before, I lived many of my years as a professing Christian. There were many trials that came my way. I remember one particular time when my ex husband had committed a crime that landed him in jail. I prayed and prayed for God to take him out of the situation and let him be able to get out of jail and not go to prison. On the day of his trial, my brother and mom came with me to make sure I would be ok. As the judge read over his charges, it sounded like there may be a glimmer of hope that would allow room for him to make it home. It didn't happen that way. He was sentenced to a year in prison. Looking back, it was truly God because with the seriousness of the charges, he could've gotten a much steeper sentence, but God showed mercy. You couldn't tell me that at the time. I was angry with God. I was so mad that all I could do was cry. My mother and brother tried to console me, but I told them, "Don't tell me all of that biblical stuff." The trial of facing living life alone had left me stunned and alone. In my lack of relationship with the Father, I felt that anything I prayed for should've been answered right away. How could He not answer me? This again showed the true selfishness of my nature. I was angry like a child having a tantrum, all because God didn't do what I wanted him to do. He had a greater plan for me, one that would change my life, but I couldn't see past my own desires. I was so deceived. The problem with deception though, is that you aren't able to see how deeply it runs until you step out of it. Thank You Jesus for opening my eyes.

Thank God for the trials that I faced because being alone and having so many obstacles ran me right into the hands of God. He changed me and I was renewed in the mind of Christ. During those trials, I found solace in Christ. When my ex husband went to jail, I was so sad that I had been "duped" by my faith in God. Nonetheless there was so much going on. I myself had a mother who was hospitalized. She had been in the hospital with a stent placement and it went terribly wrong. She ended up in a coma on a breathing machine. I prayed and prayed. I even sought out my Pastor, who at the time, was unaware and uncaring about my situation with my mom and my then husband. One young lady who attending my former church seen how distraught I was one Sunday, when I was trying to seek out my Pastor to pray over my oil so I could pray for my mother. She came and she encouraged me to go to God for myself. She told me that the same God that would bless the oil if I was giving it to my former Pastor, would be the same one who would bless it if I had prayed. She also came to the hospital with me and prayed over my mother. God revealed that my mom was scared and she needed us to be there. We (3 of 5 of her children) agreed to take turns but in the end it was God and me. I cried and prayed and read the word to her. Being that my ex husband had went to prison, I could devote all of my time to my mother and praying over her and spending time making sure she was okay. Prior to that time, I had been so preoccupied with my husband and his many affairs that I could not even begin to focus the way that I was able to then. When she came out, she wanted me to come to church with her. I obliged. It changed my life. On the first day that we visited the church, my Pastor had called everyone who would to come to the altar. Before I could protest, I was in the front of the church. His instructions were simple. He wanted us to pray silently to God about whatever we desired. He told us he would touch and agree with it. I prayed subvocally to God about my then husband, my father and my brother being in jail. I wanted God to free them. There was no way that my Pastor would have known what I prayed outside of God's revelation. He came near and whispered the words, "God bring her loved ones home." At that moment, I knew that God had sent me to that church. It has been my church for 11 years now. God had used a horrible situation to not only rebuild my relationship with my mother, but to build me. If I didn't have God in my life, I would've truly lost my mind. Authentic Christians are able to go through their trials and no matter what the look of the situation, they can lean on the Word of God and find assurance. Authentic Christians are able to take God's Word at face value and see a way out beyond the closed doors and mountains that have to be moved. What I learned from those difficult times was something that can not be given a value. I learned the truth of being an authentic Christian. Dear reader, if you have not yet become committed fully to Jesus Christ, and find yourself wavering in your faith, I encourage you to commit today. You will never find peace in God any other way.

Chapter 5: The "Good" Of This World

They say hindsight is 20/20. This is becoming more and more true the older I get. Going back to my teen years, I look back on my thoughts, motivations, and plans and none of them involved anyone's happiness but my own (especially not God's). My desires were to be a lawyer, to marry my high school sweetheart, to have lots of children and to be very successful in life. These are goals of many teen girls, planning out the perfect wedding, naming their children before they even get pregnant. Silly things that girls do. I felt no different than the average teen. This in itself was error as well. I attended church and I was involved with ministry all the time. I would attend Christian faith meetings in school, pray, and talk about God often. In the world's view, I was a responsible teenager who was aware of my desires and willing to go for my dreams. Additionally, I actually believed God and was willing to share the gospel (if needed) and I was a GOOD child. You may be reading this and thinking this sounds fine. I thought the same thing. This brings to heart the scripture in Proverbs 14:12

There is a way which seems right unto a man, but the end thereof are the ways of death.

Therein lies the problem. The world has it's own version of what good is and it doesn't line up with what God's standard of good is. In the world to be driven and motivated towards whatever it is that makes you happy is something that most applaud. The world encourages you to take a look at your life, find out WHAT YOU WANT and go after it with all that you have. "You control your destiny" is something that I have heard time and time again, and to be honest that is true. God has given us a free will that allows us to choose what we want to follow, to choose either His way or the world's way. However, that bible verse scares me. I mean, it's one thing to do the wrong thing and then death comes, but to be thinking that you are doing the right thing and then death comes is completely different. I didn't want to be in that position. Nevertheless I was in fact there. See, beyond our world, there is a God who does everything with a purpose. Nothing God does is just because. That definitely includes His creation of you and me. I know this because of verses like Jeremiah 1:5 which states:

Before I formed you in the womb I knew you, before you were born I set you apart; I appointed you as a prophet to the nations."

This bible verse reveals to us that God has an intimate relationship with us even before we are brought forth in our mother's womb. It reveals that He chooses us and ordains us long before we even know ourselves. If He has appointed us in a particular service to Him, who are we to try and decide what it is that we want to do with our lives? If He has formed us and created us in a certain nature, who are we to say that we desire to be something different? I remember I loved being in those career choice activities and they would ask me all types of questions about my preference. My favorite questions were about how I think and things that I like to do. Often those tests would reveal my strengths. I would take so much pleasure in being told what things were good about me. All of this was vanity. God was not pleased in any of it. See, when He created me, He knew my strengths, because He is the One who gave them to me. When He formed me, He knew my weaknesses, because He used them to build my character. I had taken it upon myself to find out my path in life when the bible clearly states in Proverbs 3:5-6

***Trust in the Lord with all your heart,
And lean not on your own understanding;
In all your ways acknowledge Him,
And He shall direct your paths.***

I adore the Word of God because it makes things so clear. If you take the time to search the scriptures and look at the mindset that God is directing us to have, you would be able to see that the ways that the world prescribe are far from it. In leaning on our own understanding of who we are and what we are destined to do, one is quickly breaking this instruction from God. If in fact you are leaning on our own ways (the ways of the world), you are not acknowledging Him in all your ways. The world has pushed God out of the equation of our life and made Him of none effect in our choices and our decisions. Nonetheless if we want to be successful, we must get back to the basics of seeking Him for all of our needs and relying on Him to be our guide. No career quiz or guidance counselor can tell you what you were created to do.

There are those who are blinded by the world and continue to seek the things the world has to offer. Even if they attend church and do all the "good" that the world tells us that we should, they will be among those locked out of the kingdom of God. Our deception in even believing in any of us have any inherent good in us is foolish. Jesus Himself was approached by a young man in Mark 10.

Now as He was going out on the road, one came running, knelt before Him, and asked Him, "Good Teacher, what shall I do that I may inherit eternal life?" So Jesus said to him, "Why do you call Me good? No one is good but One, that is, God.

Jesus, who is the Son of God, is part of the Trinity and lived without sin. Nevertheless He quickly corrected the young ruler about calling Him good. How is that we, as sinful creatures who make mistakes everyday wear the label of good? Jesus reminded this young man, who was sincere in his observation of the conduct of Jesus, that only God is good. Once you think about this truth, it makes you wonder about how many times you have mistaken good for evil. I remember many times when I was going through hard times, maybe someone had wronged me or made me feel less than good and I was so hurt and angry. I would say, "I am a good person, I don't deserve this." In my way of thinking, I really didn't and that is not to say that people should be able to hurt me or mistreat me in any way, but it does humble me. Beloved, pride is not always open and puffed up, sometimes it is wrapped in deception and thinking too highly of yourself. The fact that we look at ourselves as "good" can lead us away from God and into selfishness. This is what Paul warned the Romans about in Romans 12:3

Because of the privilege and authority God has given me, I give each of you this warning: Don't think you are better than you really are. Be honest in your evaluation of yourselves, measuring yourselves by the faith God has given us.

This is a great warning because sometimes we as humans are not truly honest in our evaluation of ourselves. When I considered myself good, I only saw the "bad" in others. I couldn't see any wrong that I had done. For example, there were a few times in my life when someone I was dating would cheat on me, or behave in a deceptive way. Follow me now, I was in no way perfect, in all of my relationships I was going against the Word of God in having premarital sex and even at times living in an unmarried situation. Some of that time I was active in ministry and living in complete sin. Nevertheless, the cheating and lying on their part overshadowed my own wrongdoing. The time came to pray about **my** situation (as a Christian, I knew enough to pray). I would only pray about how bad **I** felt, and how that person had done **me** wrong, and how **I** needed God to help **me** to heal. In reality, I was desperately in need of salvation and for the scales on my eyes to be removed. I was at fault because I was in sin from the moment I consented to, better yet, entertained sexual immorality. Moreover, because I was the one who had a relationship and a commitment to be kept to God, I was even more at fault than my unsaved partner. It was only a matter of time before I got hurt, either by my partner, or my own actions because I was involved in sexual immorality. I will explain more about this later in the book.

I am reminded of Isaiah, who upon seeing the holiness of God, was immediately humbled and cried out to the Lord:

In the year that King Uzziah died, I saw the Lord sitting on a throne, high and lifted up, and the train of His robe filled the temple. Above it stood seraphim; each one had six wings: with two he covered his face, with two he covered his feet, and with two he flew. And one cried to another and said:

"Holy, holy, holy is the Lord of hosts; The whole earth is full of His glory!" And the posts of the door were shaken by the voice of him who cried out, and the house was filled with smoke. So I said: "Woe is me, for I am undone! Because I

am a man of unclean lips, And I dwell in the midst of a people of unclean lips; For my eyes have seen the King, The Lord of hosts."

In the presence of God, Isaiah was able to see his own shortcomings. I believe that is true for any person who is truly in the vicinity of God's majesty and beauty. God is Holy, He is powerful and His glory is so amazing, (do you ever feel like a word you use to describe God is insufficient?). His majesty creates a feeling of awe that is indescribable. I imagine that when Isaiah saw such perfection and staggering breathtaking magnificence, He could do nothing else but humble Himself. His words are so powerful, "Woe is me, I am undone". In truth, previous chapters of Isaiah involved him judging other people. (Isaiah 5). However when He saw the majesty of God, and caught a glimpse of his true holiness, he felt ruined, like all of the "good" he had once felt was melted away by the power of the One True God. I remember last year my family and I were planning a trip to go Black Friday shopping. I was so tired that morning, I rushed to get dressed and threw on any clothes I could find. My hair was not even combed into place, as I felt "well, we're just going shopping, *who will pay attention?*" I got in the car feeling pretty okay about how I looked until I came to the shopping outlet. There were so many people, and they all had on pretty decent clothing. I looked in the mirror in one of the stores and wanted to run out. That messy hair looked like a wild woman when I saw others with hairs all in place. My quick "throw on" dress looked just that, thrown on. I was so ashamed. When you look at the hearts of many in the world who truly believe that they are flawless, it reveals the depth of their deception. We are imperfect beings made in the image of a perfect God. The bible even describes our bodies as corruptible. How then could we ever be fooled into believe that we are flawless when our very nature is sin? There is no good in us, aside from God and He alone is good.

This truth is not to make anyone lose their sense of self worth, but to empower each person with the knowledge and reference to the good that is found in God alone. I often tell my followers, "If you see anything in me that is good, then it's God. If you see anything that is in me that is flawed and corrupt, that's me." It is only when I take away the pride that this world places in us through falsehood of evil being called good that I am able to accept my need for a savior. The truth of the matter is that we need God, more today than yesterday and only half as much as tomorrow. Without leaning on Him to lead and guide us into our eternity, we are hopeless. However, when we place our hope in Him, and put our pride aside to face our true fallen nature, we are more than conquerors. I am not ashamed to say that without God, I am nothing. If it wasn't for His grace carrying me through every season of my life, the enemy would have destroyed me a long time ago. I thank God for His love, for His mercy and His grace. I thank God for continually blessing and keeping me. I thank God for each and every one of you, who are reading this and gaining the revelation you need in life to be prepared for eternity!

Prelude to Rage (Raegina)...

You are about to read a story about Raegina, who is a Christian. She is very active in ministry. She is the daughter of a Pastor, and leader of several ministries within her church. Like many Christians today, Raegina believes that the validity of her walk with Christ is interrelated with the amount of work she does in the church. Raegina is smart, beautiful, and very dedicated to the work that she does in ministry. Some of the things in Raegina's life may remind you of things that happen in your own walk with Christ. Keep in mind that everything that occurs to Raegina is biblically based. While reading about Raegina, I would like for you to take the time to highlight all of the things that you have in common with Raegina, as well as those things that stick inside your heart as you read, as they may be things that the Holy Spirit wants to deal with you about. Also, please take the time to reference the scriptures in this book as they will give you clarity on the truth. The bible tells us, **"Then will you know the truth, and the truth will set you free."** Some of this section of the book will be quite honestly shocking. It was hard for me as a believer to face the hard truth of what awaits those who are in fact, turned away from

Jesus Christ. I dare you to challenge your heart and mind, as compare the revelations in this chapter of the book with the things that Jesus has to say about eternity. For a long time, I was afraid to read the book of Revelation, or to take the time to understand what the Spirit of the Lord was saying to the churches. However, now is the time for each one of us to face the truth. It is my greatest desire that as you read this story, you will experience the truth and He will set you free!

Chapter 6: The Twinkling of an Eye

"He's not married, just dating...it's not adultery." I had to tell myself this at least a dozen times when he was around. I rolled over and kissed his shoulder. He stirred, then opened one eye and smiled. "Girl, you were so wild last night." Embarrassed on what may have taken place, I just smiled coyly. To be honest I didn't remember. It was my girl Lexie's bday party and we had hit the club. I wore this cute one piece that made Lexy scream with excitement when I showed it to her. "You are NOT wearing that!!!" I just smiled at her. Hell, we were in a whole nother town... Nobody would know it was me in this Beyonce get up. My fur coat covered me a lil piece...I felt so free in this little cute outfit. My cheeks were out, covered only by my net stockings underneath. I wore a wig that was honey blonde and my makeup was flawless. All Lexy and my entourage (as I called her corney friends in my head) could do was stare. Well, everybody did. They had never seen me in this light. All I remember was dancing, smoking plenty loud and texting Omere to come meet me at my overly expensive hotel suite that I was alone in. And he did...I promised him he wouldn't regret it cause I was on one...my guess is he didn't cause he was laying there with this stupid grin on his face. My phone vibrated and I jumped out of bed in all my naked glory to run to the restroom. He reached for me and i smiled. "Be back in 10 babe." He let go of my hand and turned over. My phone vibrated again as I sat down on the side of the Jacuzzi...

Marie: Evangelism team meeting at 6pm in the sanctuary

Sam: Gotta work tonight!

Rebecca: I will be there, hallelujah!

Steve: Lord willing I will be there.

Frances: I will be there in the presence of the Lord.

Marie: Rage, can you take lead in the meeting?

I rolled my eyes at the group text. Why do I have to head the meeting? I'm tryna chill with bae tonight....I closed out of the message app and headed back into the bedroom. He was still laying in the same spot. "Your lil girlfriend get on my nerves calling all these meetings. It's almost like she know we here and want to ruin our night..." Startled, he jumped and motioned for me to be silent. He turned his back to me and continued his phone conversation."...Nothing babe, that's the television." He was on the phone with her!!! I did everything to quiet my anger that was screaming inside of me. I walked into the bathroom and pulled out my stash of loud and was feeling better in 4 minutes. I know cause I watched the clock. He came in sniffing the air with a goofy smile on his face. My heart melted as he wrapped his arms around my waist and kissed my neck. He kissed me and my head exploded with all kinds of excitement. He grabbed me so close I couldn't breathe. I couldn't help but allow him to lead me back into the bedroom....he was my Kryptonite. I stopped before we got to the bed. I smiled at his confused face. "Lets break in that Jacuzzi.." I sauntered to the tub and smiled as he settled in behind me. Suddenly I felt the urge to get my life in order...to let go of this sinful scene and stop indulging in him. I looked into his deep green eyes and let my inhibitions and convictions go. "You only live once," I said in my head...."And I am living."

Suddenly I heard a loud blast...like so loud I was stuck. It was like it went through my body...better yet my soul. I couldn't move. It blared over and over again. I looked at Omere, hoping it was the loud and I was tripping, but his horrified face told me it was real....my heart dropped as I cried out, "No, it can't be...not now..."

Chapter 7: Hopelessness

....I was frozen...could it be that my time was up??? Nah... I tried to replay every part of the story in my head. I couldn't shake the feeling that it was all true. My time is up...I tried to pray but I felt so empty. Like why did I feel so empty??? "Jesus, Jesus..." I repeated His name but I felt so cold as I said it. The room spinned. Suddenly I snapped into the reality of Omere calling my name. "Rage! Rage! Reagina!!!" I looked up and saw him with pants on grabbing a shirt. He still had bubbles from the jacuzzi on his back. I looked down at my nude body and realized I hadn't moved a muscle. I gathered my strength and began to step out of the tub... Suddenly my back was against the floor. I had fallen. Where was my strength?? "Babe get up!" Omere handed me a dress and helped me off the floor. He dried me off as I was in a daze. "We gotta go babe..." I pulled the baby pink dress my mom gifted me for Christmas over my head and down my damp body. I walked behind him out of the bathroom, into the bedroom and out into the hall. People were crying, frantic, screaming. I was numb. All of a sudden I saw a huge ball of fire shoot through the glass of the hotel window. I snapped into my senses and began to run. Omere rushed me through the crowd. We ran down the stairs through a door and into the daylight. I squinted my eyes at the brightness of the sun. I was flabbergasted. Cars were on fire...there were people inside some of them, screaming for help. Some people were looting and news broadcasters yelled into mics. Was it an earthquake? Hardly in Daytona Beach...we were in the heart of Florida. How could it be an earthquake??? Was it a terrorist attack? I could hear the questions of everyone as I looked around and took in the chaos around me. Fire balls were falling, setting some on fire. "Rage!!!" I heard Omere as he pulled me into safety. "We have to go down into the basement or something, this ain't safe." I pulled back and looked into his eyes. We both knew what was going on...we both knew nowhere was safe...

Chapter 8: outRage

We went down a flight of steps frantically searching for a lower floor. Omere spoke first..."Let's just find the basement until it is declared safe. This mess is crazy." I stared at him, shaking my head. "Omere, you know it's over right?" His eyes said it all. He was shaken, the life in his eyes had faded. He rubbed his wavy hair...his back was to me. I felt a single tear fall down my cheek. "I knew what those sounds were when we were upstairs. He came back, Jesus came back and took His people that were prepared." Omere turned around... His face was cold and menacing. I was afraid of his demeanor. Startled...I backed away. "It wasn't supposed to be like this!! I am a MINISTER. I'm supposed to be with my fiancé!!! I stood shocked at his statement. He launched towards me, placing his hands around my neck as he screamed out obscenities at me. I never knew he hated me...I thought we were in love. I tried to pull his hands away from my throat. He was so strong! I fell on the cold cement and he straddled me still choking me. I felt anger rise in me like a kindling fire as I reached for something, anything to get him off me. I felt something like a brick and I grabbed it. I hit him as hard as I could. I felt cold. Blood dripped from his head on my lip. I pushed him off me. He fell on the ground gripping his head and looking at me with the most hateful Iook I have ever seen outside of horror movies. I looked down at my dress. Blood was all over my pink dress. I screamed at the top of my lungs..."What in the HELL is going on???" Behind my scream I heard a cackle of laughter. I turned around to see a woman emerge from the back of me. Her eyes were haunting. She reeked of what I assumed was urine. "Hell is what is going on..." she laughed, her cackle filling the entire room. Fear overcame me. I was so scared. Scared and angry. She laughed harder. "I mean, here you are, fornicating with your sister's fiance and your savior has come and gone.." Now I was even more angry. I grabbed her and pulled her by her tattered shirt. "What is your problem?? What the hell is wrong with you?" she laughed harder. I must admit I wanted to ram her head into the wall. Who was she to air out my dirty laundry? Then I wondered how did she know. Omere stood up, dazed as I pushed her into the wall. I was ready to pick up a brick and beat him repeatedly. How dare he not tell me he had asked my sister to marry him? Here I am giving him all of me, letting him do whatever he wanted to me however and whenever while she was a "virgin" who refused to even consider a man's desires and he would marry her. I grabbed the brick and busted him in his face. More blood. It fueled me even more. I hit him one, two, ten times. I lost count. It felt good. I stood up over his lifeless body and I laughed. Laughed like the cackling woman who had somehow disappeared. "Reagina Dubois" I heard my name and walked towards the voice automatically in a robotic fashion.

Chapter 9: Numbness Following

My name had been called. I knew I needed to head in the direction of the voice. Numbness filled my being, as I walked up the stairs and towards the door. "Rage".. It was Omere's voice calling me from downstairs. I knew for a fact that he shouldn't be able to breathe, let alone call my name after I hit him that many times. But somehow, it didn't bother me at all. Nothing mattered. I swung open the door that lead to the street. Silence. I should have been confused but I knew that this is how it was supposed to be. "Raegina Dubois, you are being summoned to the sanctuary." I turned around to see a very handsome man. His face shined like day in the midst of darkness. He looked peaceful. I almost spoke to ask him about who he was but something inside of me knew not to speak. I walked into a huge building with the most beautiful decor I had ever seen. The floors were like golden glass, every window glistened like diamonds. There were so many people. Many I knew, and even more I didn't know. They all looked as confused as I was. Every person who stood near the doors had a similar countenance to the young man whom I had seen heading into what I knew as the sanctuary. Then it hit me. If I was in fact about to stand before Jesus in the sanctuary, then it means my sins are forgiven. After all, I was assistant to the head of my evangelical team at church. I taught over 200 children in youth ministry and I even taught dance and piano in the church's after school program. Prior to this last wild night with Omere, I was preparing to go on a Daniel fast with the kids to welcome in the new year. My father was the Pastor of the church. And prayers of the righteous availeth much. I knew he was praying for me. Although I was a little confused about how the entire rapture happened, I was sure of God's mercy. I could feel myself gaining assurance in my salvation as I noticed the room had paired off into 2 groups. One went into the room on the left and one went into the room on the right. Then I noticed the gentleman from earlier. I smiled. He motioned for me to go to the room on the right. I quickly was ushered in and the huge golden door closed behind me. I looked around the room. I saw Sister Wendell who was over the finances at church, Brother Morissette who was over the prison ministry was there. I felt relieved. They both were very faithful to the church. For some reason, we all knew not to talk. I thought about how it would be to stand before Jesus. To see His grace, behold Him and be in His presence. Just then, I remembered my blood stained dress. I looked down and noticed that I had on white.

Not the brilliant white the gentleman who had let me in, but I figured that I would receive my white after I see Jesus. All of a sudden, I heard my name being called again. I walked toward the voice...my heart raced as the golden doors opened and I headed towards the 2nd set of doors that lead to Him...

Chapter 10: Amazement in Despair

The doors opened and I held my breath. The room was even larger than the previous one. The ceiling wasn't visible...just light illuminated from all around it seemed. There was a throne with a body of water that looked like it was made of jewels in front of it. I saw creatures full of eyes. They were so beautiful and strange I turned away. They repeatedly cried, "Holy, Holy, Holy..." The room held people on both sides and there was an aisle that lead to the throne. I finally saw what they meant by streets made of gold. It glistened under my feet. It was so beautiful. Something inside of me rumbled. I didn't want to look at what was ahead of me. I stopped walking, looking around to see if I could find a familiar face in the crowd...someone who would assure me it would be fine. I seen Abigail, the little girl who was like 17, who worked at the homeless shelter standing in the crowd. I knew her because I had volunteered there a few times. She was always so helpful, even asking for donations to clothe the kids and to help some of the parents from the shelter get bus fare. I don't know why, but she seemed so much more beautiful. She shined, much like the handsome gentleman I had seen earlier. I wondered if I was allowed to say hello, but I decided against it. Almost as if she knew I wanted to talk, she came to me and smiled. "Hello Raegina, I want to thank you for all that you did for the shelter." Confused, I smiled. I felt angry at how happy she was. She continued, "Because of your giving, many of the people from the shelter have been given a crown, and have entered into the joy of the Lord." She smiled again and walked back into the crowd, which had become a sea of faces. I felt a tap on my shoulder and fear flooded my mind and soul. I slowly turned around to see Lexy. She was so different. Her hair was like silk, it shined like the lights all around me. Her smile was perfect, and she had that same peace I felt with Abigail and that gentleman I had seen earlier. I was angry immediately, and would have punched her if I could. "Rage, the day is here. God has forgiven me for my sins! I am so glad I started my prayer closet time like you told me!!! I was in the closet when He came..." Her voice echoed in my head as I remembered what I was doing at the moment the trumpets sounded. I felt even more angry...jealousy, and envy caused me to snatch away from her and walk in the opposite direction. Lexy had been forgiven. She wasn't even saved when I met her. She was loose, loved to sleep around with men and women. I met her while I was handing out tracts at an abortion clinic. I helped her gain knowledge about God and somehow she made it. As I walked away, I felt a mix of emotions. Fear, anger, and something powerfully dark was present in my heart. I walked toward the aisle and begin my journey to the throne. I saw even more familiar faces. I dared not speak to them to hear their wonderful testimony of God's grace. I just wanted to be forgiven. Then we could rejoice together. Suddenly I heard a scream so loud I stopped my thoughts of coveting and looked ahead. A familiar voice...Omere!!! I ran ahead and looked...he was being hauled away into a door on the left. He cursed God's name...the look in his eyes was even darker than I had seen before. He was kicking, so violent that his whole body looked as if he was having convulsions. The door swung open and I saw darkness I had never seen before. It was heat so hot it felt as if my face was singed. I felt like I was the only one in the room at that moment. Everyone else had disappeared. "Reagina Dubois, come forward." My legs were moving as if on their own and finally I looked up. I saw Him. His face was stern, yet loving. His light was indescribable. No picture I had seen on earth, nor imagination in my heart could mirror His beauty. I saw power in Him, majesty, holiness. He looked at me and through me. I knew He knew all of my faults. He sat like the King of Kings. I wanted to hide just looking at Him. I noticed Him looking through His book and became afraid...He closed it and looked me in the eyes...

Chapter 11: King of Kings

Jesus looked in my eyes and I saw.. better yet I felt the love He had for me. However, deep down I knew that love would not overshadow His word that stated all liars and fornicators would enter into the hell fire. I shuddered within my soul at this thought. He had more compassion than I have ever felt as He told me, "Your name is not written in the book of life." Immediately, an angel began to look through a huge stack of books. I wanted to run... hide... scream... maybe even get another chance to make the right choice like in movies. Perhaps I could even get another chance like I had a thousand times before after awakening from a vision of this day. I couldn't believe just 24 hours ago I felt I had all the time in the world to repent. It wasn't fair...my mom, dad, grandma and all those who raised me saying "Jesus is coming soon," for years had so many years of sinning behind them and had time to repent. Why was I robbed of that time? I mean, it sounds selfish but really. Didn't all the good I did matter? I have taught 200 plus children stories about Him, His law, His instructions. I had over 300,000 facebook followers and over 700,000 podcast viewers who listened to my prayer and biblical instruction weekly. I was second in command to the evangelism team. We have given to the poor, petitioned to end abortion, visited prisons, the hospitals...my work was solid. I mean, God knows my heart was set to serve Him and I did. I slipped up on Omere...but I didn't know it would end so horribly. Plus the time I waited for a husband like my 'holier than thou' tramp sister, God sent nobody my way. Unless you count Rodney, the church playboy who wanted everyone secretly and nobody openly. I thought it was love, even prayed for marriage but pretty soon it was apparent he was sleeping with me and numerous other women who were as naive as I was. I had believed he was a true man of God who had lost his way. I had repented of that sin and was reconciled to God when Andre came along. He was also a Sunday school teacher who I had fell so hard for that we even had a few indiscretions in my daddy's church. He had let me down in a major way. One day I walked into a room with him in the bed with his 'best friend since high school'. Crazy thing is my daddy told me that Andre was homosexual. I didn't listen. Dating a down low man had really revealed to me that I needed God. I repented of that too, so I know I am not held accountable for that fiasco. I felt myself getting angry at the fact that my name had been left out of the book. Very angry. So angry that I was about to be like my phone on 0% and go off. Suddenly, I felt this presence in front of me. I say felt because I didn't actually see her but I knew she was right in front of me, directly between me and Jesus. I got this feeling she was so familiar. My heart plummeted as I realized it was my life standing there, ready to testify of how I had spent every moment of every day...

Chapter 12: Life's Story

I stood there...mortified at the fact that there was nothing I could do. My life was literally living proof of my fallacies. I realized I was holding my breath and I exhaled. My life unfolded like a curtain. The first scene was my birth. My dad and mom were so young and happy. I almost smiled until I heard my dad make the declaration he had always made..."My beautiful Raegina Nichole Dubois...you have been created to bring the news of the gospel to the nations." I rolled my eyes. My dad would often make this proclamation with so much joy and expectation in his voice. I mean, yeah it's sweet the first few times you hear it. But after 23 years, it's plain redundancy. The next scenes were various milestones, my baby dedication, my various dance ministering when I was 4-7. Then it displayed a particular scene when I was 10 years old. My mom dad, sister and I had stopped at a Chinese restaurant for my birthday. Inside, my parents let me order whichever dish I desired. I chose many different delicacies and was heading to the car when we saw a homeless man living on the street. My dad took the time to explain homelessnes. I was compelled to walk over to the older man and give him my food. "God has not forgotten you. I pray that My Father provides for you and gives you perfect health.

I pray for you to be saved in Jesus name. Amen." I got up and walked away. My parents, who were in tears, turned back to go into the restaurant to replace my food I had so selflessly given away and I refused. I told them that I wanted to fast for this man to be saved. My daddy wept openly and hugged me. It became one of his favorite stories to tell about me. When I saw this scene, though, I rolled my eyes. I personally thought, "that was very naive of me." Until I saw the very same man, nodding and smiling in the crowd. His face shone just like Abigail and Lexy. His skin, once full of scars and blemishes, was absolutely flawless. I noticed the gentleman who had informed me earlier of me being summoned suddenly standing next to me again. "God remembered your sacrifice and prayer. Years later, this man gave his life to Jesus Christ because of your prayer for his salvation." I was shocked. I looked again at the man who stood in the crowd and back to the man who spoke to me. "By the way, I am Josiah, your guardian angel." I couldn't believe my ears. After years of hearing my daddy preach about guardian angels, here I was standing next to mine. The scenes continued to play before me and I was too proud of my younger self. Giving away clothing, toys, being obedient to my parents...I was good until it got to my 13th year. The first scene was when I attempted to steal my daddy's new Mercedes. It was a winter night and I had told my then 20 year old church drum playing boyfriend that I would sneak out to see him. I didn't know anything about driving. I waited until about 12:30 a.m. and I grabbed the keys from the counter and snuck out the front door. Upon entering the car, I realized daddy had parked in front of mommy's car. I would have switched keys but mom's Volvo wasn't anything compared to the sleek black 2006 Benz my daddy had. I decided to attempt to move the car by backing up at an angle to get it out. Trouble was, I didn't see the pole. I hit it...hard. The car was damaged and I couldn't do anything but pull my dad's now damaged car back into the spot. I went back into the house, got a sharp knife and cut up his seats, steering wheel and left the passenger door ajar so he would think it was vandalism. It worked. So well that this was the first time it had been exposed. I looked away. I felt my stomach cringe with the next scenes, each one exposing my numerous sexual partners, my heavy drinking and smoking (many times being under the influence ministering). Finally, my 2 abortions I had never told anyone about flashed before the entire room. I wanted my life to stop...it was too much to bear. But it kept playing on and on.....

Chapter 13: Obedience > Sacrifice

My life had revealed so much of my story that I couldn't bear to even hold my head up. My life had shown the intimate details of my every secret. My sister's high school sweetheart had gotten me pregnant at 15. I seduced him at a party and poked holes in the condom. I wanted him to choose me. Once I told him I was pregnant, he moved away. Ashamed, I aborted the baby and never told a soul. My second abortion was from a guy who my sister dated in college. I had stalked him via facebook until I tracked down his favorite hangouts and hooked up with him. After a few sexcapades I revealed I was Marie's younger sister. He was horrified. He told me he didn't know what kind of games I was playing but he wanted no parts of it. He stopped dating my sister and everything. Problem was I was pregnant again. I immediately aborted. Truth be told, this was one of the main reasons I petitioned at the clinic. I figured God would forgive me if I helped others. I had never truly repented for these hidden sins. By the time my life had revealed Omere, my hidden agenda of sabotaging my sister was crystal clear. While I had originally felt that the good I did would overshadow the bad, the complete opposite had come true. All my nights I would buy liquor and get super drunk, my many sex partners, my competition I held with not only my sister, but with others was laid out. My life had shone light on my every thought, motive, and intent. Even the times when I gave to the poor, I was so quick to broadcast it on my Facebook and my podcast that there was no reward left for me in Heaven. I had no more confidence in anything I did. No more hope that perhaps my years of attending church and leading ministries would help me to make it into heaven. To be honest, it made me seethe in anger. This judgment day sucked. I may as well have spent more time smoking and drinking and partying if this was how it would end. I should've just did whatever I wanted to do. "You did". Startled, I looked up at the throne. The words Jesus spoke had sent waves of shock in my body. I forgot He could hear my thoughts. "You did everything you wanted to do Raegina." His face still radiated love, compassion. He was so majestic. I protested, " Lord, I attended church every Sunday, I...." Jesus' powerful voice interjected me. "You attended church every Sunday and you COMPLAINED EVERY SUNDAY MORNING about having to go. You did your ministries half-heartedly. Although I sent many to you for you to help, you completely ignored them if they were not as flashy as you, or didn't admire you enough. You judged others by how much money they put in the collection plate. You chose friendship at the church based on their looks, and financial status. You isolated those who you felt 'weren't good enough' for you. Many people came and left your church because of your lack of compassion towards them. Even when they left, you would talk against them and make no efforts to change your approach in ministry. You made jokes of people's flaws instead of praying for them. When your brothers and sisters in Me went through trials you would gossip about their pain. People who had trusted and confided their faults in you were betrayed by you, as you would tell others of their faults and judge them with no intentions of coming to Me to intercede for them. Beloved, don't you remember my second greatest commandment? Thou shalt love thy neighbor as thyself. " I felt my heart sank...I felt a wave of anger build up. I was being treated unfairly! I tried to open my mouth to speak but couldn't. Jesus clearly had the floor right now...I knew that what He had to say would shape where I spent my eternity...

Chapter 14: Lost Souls

I shuddered at the thought of what was coming next. My eyes burned with the anticipation of tears. I didn't even want to look at Jesus. I was sure I would see the same level of disappointment I saw in my mother's eyes when she walked in while I was sleeping with the thug from the corner. I imagined He would have the look my father had when he found out that I had completely disregarded my vow of chastity long before my 16th birthday. Perhaps even the look my sister had when she found out I had slept with 2 out of 4 of her boyfriends (when secretly it was all 4 but I was too ashamed to let her know). Instead, the unconditional love He held for me was still in His eyes. This somehow angered me. I don't know why. "Raegina, your assignment has been to gain souls for the kingdom. However, your life has been consumed with pursuing your own lusts and disregarding all that I have called you to do. You have set a standard of lukewarmness in your life in which you balanced worldliness with holiness. You never truly chose to follow me wholeheartedly. You were never loyal... not to your friends, not to your family, but most importantly, not to Me. You hated your sister because she truly chose holiness. You set your heart against her to destroy her. What you failed to understand is that when I am for her, no weapon formed against her would prosper. I protected you, called to you, gave you chance after chance. Somehow, you felt that you were entitled to an eternity in Heaven when in reality you were unable to live 23 years of holiness. This proves you are unworthy to experience eternity in the holy of holies." Jesus looked over towards the beautiful angels standing near the throne. "How many souls were assigned to Raegina?" "182,532 directly and 516,982 through others." I stood there surprised at these numbers. "That's impossible!!" I screamed! "I don't even know that many people! Your standards are way too high!". Jesus remained calm and stated, "My beloved Raegina, My grace is sufficient. Had you simply humbled yourself and asked Me for grace to obey My commandments, I would have provided you with My Holy Spirit. With Him you would have overcome every obstacle in your life and lived holy before Me always." I interjected, "But Lord, how? How could I have possibly reached that many souls?" Jesus stated with so much love, "With man it is impossible, but with God all things are possible." He looked to the angel again and asked, "How many souls did she reach?" the angel looked in the book and stated "185 directly and 3,348 through others." Jesus looked back at me and the love was not erased, but sadness was very apparent. I knew what was coming next, yet nothing could prepare me for it....

Chapter 15: Final Destination

Jesus' sheer power and His love for judgment radiated as He sat there in all His glory. I knew I had failed miserably and it was no denying it. I must express this again, Jesus' love never diminished. Even in all this revelation about my horrid secrets, the love I felt generated from Him did not lessen. This is because He sees all and knows all. Nothing was ever hidden from Him. However, I could see that it hurt Him to see me make such bad choices. "Raegina, not only have you created a mass of sin in your life, but you have lead others into deception." Now I was completely confused. "Jesus, I don't understand." Jesus looked at me once again, sadness and love filled His expression. "Raegina, I entrusted you with many souls via Facebook and your podcast. You had the duty of leading the lost to Me. However, because of your carelessness many of them have been led to lukewarmness and hypocrisy." I felt angry again. I was guilty of many things but this was too much!! "How is that possible, Jesus? I never *intentionally* told someone to sin." My life didn't miss a beat. She quickly revealed numerous Facebook posts and podcasts. Some of them I didn't even remember. Some were vaguely familiar. Many of them were random posts I had made when I was drunk or high expressing my feelings at the moment. "But Lord, I don't understand." Jesus spoke with so much strength and wisdom. "My people are destroyed for lack of knowledge. Do you not understand that I assigned souls to you? These souls are connected to you through business relationships, social media, friendships, and familial relationships. As a Christian, you should understand that people watch everything you do. You are the living example of my Word. You are called to pick up your cross to follow Me by sacrificing the ways of this world and living by My standard set in My Word. When you carelessly posted worldly statuses and podcasts that glorified the world and things in it like clothes, money, career moves and social status, you neglected the things of God. This led others to do the same because they looked up to you for spiritual guidance. When you belittle them or act contrary to My word, you turn them not only away from My church but from Me." Jesus turned to the angels and asked, "How many people have entered hell because of her posts?" The angel reported 4,023. Jesus' face began to look stern again. "Raegina Nichole Dubois, you have been lukewarm in all of your ways. You have made a friendship with the world which has made you an enemy of Me. I have sent prophets, visions, and even ministers of your own household to draw you unto Me, yet you rebelled. You lived your life fulfilling all your lusts and desires. Greater still, you have lead many astray through your inconsistencies and fallacies. You have lied, fornicated, committed backbiting, gossiping, and have been unrepentant in all your ways. Therefore you have chosen to make your eternal abode in hell." I literally choked at His final words. Anger filled me like never before. How dare He!!! I lashed out, "How??? After all I have done for your kingdom!!! How dare you banish me to hell just because I couldn't live up to your impossible standard you set??" Jesus looked through my being and stated words I never wanted to hear. "Depart from me, I never knew you." At this point I lost all control. I kicked and screamed. I wanted to charge at him. The love I once thought I had for him transformed into pure hatred. I began to curse him in words I had never used. He still looked at me in love and compassion mixed with sadness. Immediately, I was escorted through the door I had seen Omere dragged through in the same manner. I was using the same vulgar words filled with a hatred originated from the darkest corners of hell. No longer could I say I was a child of God. I was as wicked as satan himself, as God's presence was forfeited when I chose worldly pleasures over God's promises and eternity provided through Jesus Christ. But this was only the beginning of my worst nightmare....

Chapter 16: The Eternal Abode of Rage...

They drug me into hell and left me to burn. It seemed crazy, but the further I was drug away from Jesus, the colder my heart had become. I was angry...so angry I wanted to kill. Immediately Romans 1:18-32 popped into my mind and I growled like a beast in anger towards His Word. I imagined on earth that in hell you wouldn't be so aware of what was going on around you but truly I was wrong. The first thing that hit me was the smell. If you could imagine roadkill covered in fecal matter and rotten eggs stuffed up your nose, it would only begin to describe the putrid smell of hell. I heard the most terrifying screams I have ever heard in my life. Not one nor two or a hundred or thousand, but what sounded like billions of heart wrenching screams from every angle. Demonic laughter saturated me in fear. I looked at my hands it was as if they were in instant decay. I was reminded of the bible verse that stated that Jesus is the way, the truth and the life. Without Him, my body had no life...I felt powerless. I began to feel like there was no air in hell at all. I gasped and choked. I tried to inhale but all I felt was pressure on my lungs, like I was suffocating.

Instantly I remembered verses like Job 27:3 and Job 33:4 as well as Isaiah 42:5 which state that God gives us the breath of life. The heat was searing. Even my eyeballs felt like they were aflame. I felt burning starting at my ankles as I lay in a bed of searing coals. I looked down to see two demonic figures, each at least 8 foot tall dragging me like a rag doll... I tried to fight them off to no avail. Psalms 18 and Psalms 28 states that God is my strength. Without Him I was completely powerless. They were stronger than me in every way. "Which way is this one going?" I heard one ask. "To the right leg." The other replied. They were clearly enjoying dragging me through the coals which were burning every part of me. At one point, my skin slid off of my right foot and they lost hold of me. Angry at this, they blew fire which engulfed my skin and burned it like thin paper. I screamed with all of my might. I wished for death to rescue me from this pain. "Oh My God it hurts SOOO D**N BAD!!! I screamed in agony. They just laughed and laughed as if my torture bought them sheer delight. Soon my skin was intact again and they drug me further. I looked at my hand and the decayed flesh was there again. Maggots crawled in and out the holes the flaming hot coals had created. I could feel them eating tiny bits of my flesh as they moved in and out of my hand. I remembered the bible verse Mark 9:47-48 which Jesus had stated, ***"And if thine eye***

offend thee, pluck it out: it is better for thee to enter into the kingdom of God with one eye, than having two eyes to be cast into hell fire: Where their worm dieth not, and the fire is not quenched." Suddenly I realized that not only would I feel as these worms ate my flesh till it was no more, but they would probably grow as large as I am, or bigger as Jesus stated that they would not die. I tried to cry, but tears would not come. Suddenly, the demons stopped dragging me and dropped to the ground bowing and speaking in a language I had never heard. I heard a male voice stating,

"Dear Lord Jesus,

I know I am a sinner, and I ask for your forgiveness. I believe you died for my sins and rose from the dead. I trust and follow you as my Lord and Savior. Guide my life and help me to do your will.

In your name, Amen."

I looked up into the blackest darkness I had ever seen. Why would the sinner's prayer be recited in Hell? Then I saw a beautiful angel standing before me. I was so relieved...

Chapter 17: Angel of Light

This angel shined so bright, for a moment I had forgotten the tortuous scene surrounding me. He smiled, reciting the Lord's prayer again. I repeated it after Him. His face was very handsome and sculptured like a male model. He was very buff, even under his white garment you could see the cut of his chest. Was I attracted to this angel??? He smiled at me and reached out towards me. I extended my tattered hand and he was able to easily pull me up. As I repeated the last few words of the prayer, he began to laugh maniacally. Fear flooded every part of my being and before my eyes, this beautiful angel transformed to the most menacing monster I have ever seen. He picked me up over his head and thrust me to the floor. I screamed in agony as I felt my body hit the fire. "YOU FOOL!!" He shouted. "So easily persuaded that anything that appears good would be good! For such are false apostles, deceitful workers, transforming themselves into the apostles of Christ. And no marvel; for satan himself is transformed into an angel of light.

Therefore it is no great thing if his ministers also be transformed as the ministers of righteousness; whose end shall be according to their works. 2 Corinthians 11:13-15." satan stood over me, and I was ashamed that I had been fooled. Not only this moment but my entire life. He kicked me in the head as hard as he could. My body felt like I had been hit by a truck. "Oh how I remember your debates with people about the realities of hell...'Oh I don't believe a loving God would send His people to such a horrible place." Now when he stated my thoughts, it was in my exact voice. I knew now that many times when thoughts were formed in my mind, it was him **disguising himself as me.** I couldn't speak. I was just horrified beyond any describable feeling. He laughed again and looked down at me. "You are pathetic. Hell was created for me and the angels who I fooled long ago to follow me. We were kicked out of heaven and onto earth. Then God created human...IN HIS IMAGE!" His face was distorted at even speaking of man's creation. If it's possible to feel hate I truly felt how much he hated the human race. My stomach turned as this feeling was generated towards me. He continued, "So I figured, what better REVENGE than to take as many of this pathetic disgusting race with me? I mean, my fate had been sealed long ago, but man's fate is the most interesting thing. It is totally in his own hands!!! Man has free will...What's even better is I have the power to create the illusion that things of this world are more fun, more important, more of a necessity to tend to than things of eternity. So I created distractions: money, success, power, sexual immorality, greed, lust, so many things on earth that separate man from God and caused so very many to turn away from God. I also added false gods and placed people in positions of authority who challenged God's doctrine and made it appear faulty when in God there is nothing but truth. Of course, in the church I created a false sense of security. Even when a Christian was knee deep in sin, I convinced them it was no need of repentance. 'God knows your heart' was my favorite slogan. Well that and 'the devil doesn't exist." He laughed again, then looked at me with such an evil grin. "But my biggest defeat of man, has been the blending of good and evil, they gray areas. You know, the bashing of Christianity for the very principles that make it up. I would say it divided people the most. Christians know abortion, homosexuality, and fornication is a sin. But if they spoke against it, ***I called it hate***. I even created organizations for people who practiced such sin to unite against those Christians who chose to speak out against it or who tried to persuade them to come to Jesus. I fooled those who practiced such lawlessness to believe God had created them that way!!!" He laughed even harder at this. "And now you are here with me for eternity!!! No more time to repent, for hell is your eternal abode. And you are in for a treat!!! These two beautiful creatures, Regret and Self- hate as well as Loneliness and Shame will have the pleasure of torturing you for **all of eternity**. You will receive a harsher punishment here in the right leg of hell because you knew the Word of God and chose to follow only what was important to you." He lifted his hands and instantly fire spread from my feet to my head. I screamed over and over again. Then I felt Regret and Self-hate begin to pull me apart. I yelled even louder, "Please, Jesus!!! Please forgive me from all of my sins. Have mercy, Lord!" The demonic laughter continued, and again I wished for death...

Chapter 18: Too Late....

I laid there screaming in absolute pain as Regret and Self-hate tore each part of me apart. The worst part of my worst nightmare was that this would never end. Eternity was something that I had never really taken the time to understand. It is never-ending. I can't even count the minutes hours nor days. Why would I? Time doesn't change any circumstance in hell. The only thing we had in store was when hell will be tossed into the Lake of Fire. I screamed obscenities, begged for mercy, cried out to no avail. I remembered the many nights when I was on earth, I would pray and God would answer me. Although it was not always when I wanted, it was definitely on time. I remembered feeling so comforted every time the Holy Spirit would come to me and bring me peace in the midst of storms of my life. Oh if only I could go back to the days when I had opportunities to repent. How gladly I would have thrust myself on the floor on my knees and beg for forgiveness. Dear readers, if you are now thinking of a sin that you have not repented for, please take the time to repent. God is faithful to forgive! No matter how deep in sin you are, His hand is not too short to pull you out.

In the midst of regeneration (the time where our skin regrows after being burnt, eaten, ripped, or torn) I became numb. I felt so bad because I had done so many careless wrongs to my sister, defamed my daddy's name through my actions, disappointed my mother, and led many astray. The entire time, I was so convinced that I had been doing right for the kingdom. How wrong was I! God had designed me for a purpose, made sure His laws were made clear to me so I could be protected from the attacks the enemy made in order to make me fail. He gave me peace, gave me unmerited favor, and made His presence known in my life. He didn't desire for me to be in a place like this. I had chosen it through my blatant disobedience. I had continued in sin, although God had made every effort to save me from myself. I had hated my sister, because she was able to accomplish what I had not. She had made the right choices in life and jealousy and envy drove me to try to destroy her life. Had I only joined her in the walk with Christ, we would be together enjoying eternity with Christ. I would be reunited with my aborted babies forever. Now I was separated from all the people I loved forever. And for what? Now, at this moment I realized that nothing on earth is worth going to hell for. Because as I now painfully understood, this is a place of misery, depression, anguish and so much pain. I wished I could hug my dad, kiss my mom, or share a secret or two with my sister right now. I wished I had just one more chance to make it right. I longed for sweet communion with the Holy Spirit just one more time....but now it was too late....

Chapter 19: Reflection Of Rage

While Rage's story is very heartbreaking, my belief is truly that it could be any of us. To be perfectly honest, as I heard the Holy Spirit sealing her fate as I wrote, I realized that she could be me. Many aspects of her life were my life at times. If at any moment while I was living that carefree sinful lifestyle Jesus came, I would have been without excuse. My judgment, much like Rage's would have been set and there would be nothing that I could've done. Just thinking about that makes me so grateful for God's mercy in that He spared my soul. What about you? Were there things about her story that made you feel like it could've been you? Perhaps your sin isn't sexual or manipulative in nature. Maybe you have fallen short in other areas. The importance of her story is that it reveals that no matter what sin it is that you have committed, God's Word will be the ultimate judge. If your actions do not line up with His word, you too may be in a eternity of trouble.

Imagine if you can standing before the throne of God, looking Him face to face. How frightening that thought is, finally realizing that all of the things that you have learned about in church are true. There is really a true and Holy God who is ready to judge your life. Will you be 100% sure that the words He will say to you will be "Well done thy good and thy faithful servant?" Would your life be able to testify that you have been completely true to His word? Keep in mind that the Word of God is going to be what we are judged upon. I used to think that I was a good person, especially compared to the psychos in this world. I used to rationalize that even though everything I did wasn't "exactly" like God wanted me to do them, I wasn't as bad off as those who lived their life completely void of Christ. I would think of atheists and those who worshipped false gods and I truly believed that it would be them that God spoke to harshly on judgment day. Well, them and child molesters, murderers, rapists, and crooked politicians. Those were the people that would be shocked on judgment day as I skirted pass them with a huge "I told you so" grin on my face. Well, maybe not as apparent as an official "I told you so grin" but deep down I felt I would be able to say that in my heart. I was so incredibly wrong!

Looking back on everything that I used to believe about my salvation, I am reminded about the story in the bible found in Luke 18:

Also He spoke this parable to some who trusted in themselves that they were righteous, and despised others: "Two men went up to the temple to pray, one a Pharisee and the other a tax collector. The Pharisee stood and prayed thus with himself, 'God, I thank You that I am not like other men—extortioners, unjust, adulterers, or even as this tax collector. I fast twice a week; I give tithes of all that I possess.' And the tax collector, standing afar off, would not so much as raise his eyes to heaven, but beat his breast, saying, 'God, be merciful to me a sinner!' I tell you, this man went down to his house justified rather than the other; for everyone who exalts himself will be humbled, and he who humbles himself will be exalted."

I was much like the Pharisee who was in the story. Instead of comparing myself to the Word of God and facing the fact that I was coming up extremely short,

I wanted to compare myself to others, and exalt myself above. Many of us do this without even a second thought. But it would be equivalent to studying for a math test when the final exam is in Psychology. Heaven is a prepared place for prepared people. Are you prepared?

We have to renew our minds daily in the Word of Jesus Christ. No amount of works can get us saved. We must rely on the power of Jesus Christ to get us there. How do you do this?

Be Honest With Yourself

Sometimes, being honest with ourselves is the hardest thing to do. This is especially true if we hold positions in ministry or we feel as if exposing our truths will make others view us as inadequate or as failures. However, in order to get to the truth, which the bible has told us will set us free, we have to face it and confront it. Maybe your truth is that you don't even know if you are saved. If that question is on your mind, I want you to take the time to recite this prayer before you move on:

Father, I know that I have fallen short of Your Word. My sins have separated me from

You. I repent (am truly sorry) and I want to turn away from my sins and live for You. Father, please forgive me, and help me to obey Your commandments. I believe that your son, Jesus Christ, died for my sins, was resurrected from the dead on the third day, and is now at the right Hand of the Father and hears my prayer. I ask You Jesus to become the Lord of my life, to rule and reign in my heart for eternity. Please Lord, grant me the gift of the Holy Spirit to help me obey Your Word, and to do all that You command. In Jesus' name I pray, Amen."

Congratulations on the first step towards your new life. Keep in mind that this is not a magic prayer. Yes, you are saved once you accept Jesus Christ, but now you must put in action behind it. This means reading your Word, getting into a bible believing church and beginning life anew. You should pray often, fellowship with other believers and move forward on your journey towards eternity. Now also remember that many times satan will make it seem that somehow you are not saved. If you fall, get back up again, ask for forgiveness and move forward. Trust that God has heard your prayer and keep the faith!!!

There are some that have read that and are already saved. Facing your truth may mean digging deep into hidden sin. Do you lie (even little white ones)? Do you cheat people? Do you gossip? Are you like Raegina in being vengeful? Is there someone you secretly hate? Do you curse? Maybe watch pornography or masturbate? Hidden sins may not be easy to identify. I want you to take a second and ask The Holy Spirit to reveal the truth to you. Go ahead put the book down and ask Him. As He reveals these truths to you, grab a pen and paper and begin to write them down. Take your time, identifying these sins and facing them is vitally important. Once you have written them down, I want you to recite the following prayer:

Father, You told us in Your Word that if we confess our sins, You are faithful and just and will forgive us our sins and purify us from all unrighteousness. I come to you confessing my sins of _____. I ask You Father to please cleanse me and purify my heart. Renew a right spirit within me and transform me into who You have destined me to be. In Jesus name. Amen.

Chapter 20: Moving Forward

Once you have prayed this prayer, don't worry about these sins again. God is faithful to forgive you and you are no longer carrying the burden of those sins. Remember that the enemy will try to deceive you into believing that somehow these sins are still there, or that the simple act of praying a prayer will not allow you to be free from that sin. This is where your faith comes in. Faith is believing in God's word to be truth. Taking His word at face value is critical in finding peace in letting go of sin. You have to walk in His forgiveness, which is freely given to you. Just know that You and God have a contract through His Word, that will prevent you from being held captive by that sin again. Also remember the word given to us by Paul which tells us:

Galations 5:1:

Stand fast therefore in the liberty wherewith Christ hath made us free, and be not entangled again with the yoke of bondage.

What Paul is encouraging you to do is be free from the sin which held you bondage. Whichever sin it is, do not get involved with it *or anyone involved in it* (emphasis mine). Place your trust in the Lord and His ability to keep you from falling into the sinful lifestyle that has plagued you in the past. He is able to take the yearning that causes you to lean towards the sin that separates you from Him. When we decide to put God first, and trust in the power of His blood, we can walk in the righteousness of Jesus Christ with confidence and assurance in His ability to keep you. When Jesus stated, "It is finished," He meant just that. It was nothing left to be done. All the work that needed to be completed in order for each and everyone of us to live in a place of freedom from sin, from strongholds, from transgressions and unforgiveness has been complete. All we have to do is claim it and walk in it. So many of us spend years of unnecessary pain, depression and despair, dealing with sins that we sincerely believe we are trapped in when the truth is that we can be free! God desires for us to walk in that freedom each and every day and to take control over our lives. The choice is truly yours.

Take back the authority that is yours

I have heard many people say "the devil has power over me". Many testimonies in churches are filled with people attributing power to satan when he has no power over us at all. You may ask, "How is that he doesn't have power when Jesus Himself referenced him as 'prince of this World' in the Bible?" Clearly in John 14:30, Jesus stated, "Hereafter I will not talk much with you: for the prince of this world cometh, and hath nothing in me." While he may be referred to as the prince of the world, he is only deemed so because of the power that the world has given him. I don't know what part of the world you are reading this in, but I am sure that you have seen the many dangers that are surrounding us. Every day, thousands of children are being raped, molested, kidnapped and even killed. Women are killing their children either through abortion or through murder. Men are raping and killing women, children, and each other. There are many hidden sex trafficking rings that force individuals of all ages to commit sexual acts like slaves. Prostitution has become as normal as a 9-5 in some places. Sexual immorality plagues our television, radio and internet sites. The laws here in America have been changed to accommodate those who practice sexual immorality and to glorify abortion. Recreational drug use is becoming common in children at younger ages. The suicide rate for soldiers and vets is an alarming 22 soldiers in one day. Prayer has been taken out of schools. In certain parts of the country, you can get arrested for feeding the homeless. Are you getting the picture? The world we live in has been corrupt. However, we must not attribute that to satan having so much power that he takes over the minds and hearts of people and they are helpless to his control. The world's system is set up in opposition to God. This is why so much lawlessness abounds. Can one contribute all of this to satan? It definitely has his name on it! satan is referred to the prince of this world because in the course of creating so many laws that are in honor the very things that God Himself hates, and satan loves, he is chosen by this world as the leader. It would be quite foolish to say that the world is being led by God when there is so much opposition to His law. Let's look at how the government chooses it leaders. The election of President of the United States is when all of the citizens of the country's 50 states vote for members of the Electoral College, also known as electors. The Electors will then cast direct votes. These votes are called electoral votes for President. The candidate who receives the majority of electoral votes for President is then deemed to be the individual who is chosen to be in that office. Let's apply that knowledge to who is chosen to be the ruler of the world. God has plainly made His campaign known. The Bible reveals what His expectations are, how He desires for our actions, words, and even thoughts to be. He has made promises of blessings if we adhere to His commands. He has poured His love out to us plain as day. All of what He has desired of us has been mapped out: chapter by chapter, book by book. satan too, has mapped out his campaign to us. Let's remember, satan actually is a rebellious angel who thought more of himself than he should and decided that he would try to imitate God. In Isaiah 14:12-15, we are able to catch a glimpse of satan's dark plan:

> *How you are fallen from heaven,*
>
> *O Day Star, son of Dawn!*
>
> *How you are cut down to the ground,*
>
> *you who laid the nations low!*
>
> *You said in your heart,*
>
> *"I will ascend to heaven;*
>
> *above the stars of God*
>
> *I will set my throne on high;*
>
> *I will sit on the mount of assembly*
>
> *in the far reaches of the north;*
>
> *I will ascend above the heights of the clouds;*
>
> *I will make myself like the Most High."*

But you are brought down to Sheol,

to the far reaches of the pit. (Isaiah 14:12-15)

Satan clearly reveals that he will "make himself like God." This of course, is absurd because there is none like Him. Dear reader, do you understand that satan has a plan for you? He wants you to get caught up in sin and forget about your calling in Christ long enough for you to lose your life. He wants to snag your eternal promise. However, God has a plan as well. How we choose to operate in thinking, speaking and doing in this world decides our fate. Beloved seek God while there is time. Choose Him today.

So let's go on with our example and see which of the candidates the world has chosen. God, in His beautiful campaign for the hearts of the world has written His commandments. I believe his opening statement during debates would be as follows:

I am the L<small>ORD</small> thy God, which have brought thee out of the land of Egypt, out of the house of bondage. I am Alpha and Omega, the beginning and the end. Choose my way and have everlasting life. I will give you riches and glory and honor. If you ask anything in my Son Jesus's name, it shall be

given unto you. However, I need you to follow certain laws so that the world will be governed in decency and order. I have sent my Son Jesus Christ and My Holy Spirit to help you to keep my laws. There is no condemnation for you that are under my law and have made a covenant with Me. I will be faithful to you always. There is no weapon that the enemy can form against you that shall prosper and I will make even your enemies make peace with you. I will love you with an everlasting love and I will always be by your side. Here is a list of my commandments. I will not only give them to you, but I will also give you a helper, which is the Holy Spirit, to come and to assist you in being able to have all the tools you need to follow them. After your life is over, I have an eternity promised to you. The streets are made of gold. There will be no sickness, no anger, no sadness, just pure joy. There you will have a mansion and live forever with me and all of your loved ones that passed before you and were in me. All you have to do is adhere to the following commandments:

1 Thou shalt have no other gods before me.

2 Thou shalt not make unto thee any graven image, or any likeness of anything that is in heaven above, or that is in the earth beneath, or that is in the water under the earth. Thou shalt not bow down thyself to them, nor serve them

3 Thou shalt not take the name of the Lord thy God in vain; for the Lord will not hold him guiltless that taketh his name in vain.

4 Remember the sabbath day, to keep it holy.

5 Honour thy father and thy mother: that thy days may be long upon the land which the Lord thy God giveth thee.

6 Thou shalt not kill.

7 Thou shalt not commit adultery.

8 Thou shalt not steal.

9 Thou shalt not bear false witness against thy neighbour.

10 Thou shalt not covet thy neighbour's house, thou shalt not covet thy neighbour's wife, nor his manservant, nor his maidservant, nor his ox, nor his ass, nor anything that is thy neighbour's.

The room is silent and here is satan with his rebuttal.

I am satan. I have no rules, I have no regulations. I can make no promises to you about the afterlife, but I will cause you to question whether such a thing even exists. I will not ask you to commit to anything other than doing whatever you want to do. If you want to steal, be a thief! If you want to kill, do it! Have sex as much as you want, don't worry about marriage or keeping vows that were made. If you want to have a same sex relationship, that is fine with me. If you want to hate a man or woman because of the color of their skin, hey, WHO am I to stop you? My only wish is that you do as you desire. Greed is good. You have every right to pursue every desire in your heart. Who cares if the poor get poorer? Judge people by whichever standards you desire. If you want to serve another god other than the One who created this world, this is fine. I will supply you with all of the false information you need to make an alternative to this One who gives you rules to follow. As a matter fact, let me make a rule! There are no rules!!!

The end of the debate is up and everyone is ready to cast their votes. Now if you are honestly looking at the state of the world that we live in, it is easy to see that satan has by far won the majority. The world itself has chosen to follow the rebellious ways of satan and to let go of God's rule.

You may then in fact wonder how it is that you are supposed to take back your authority if the world itself has been following satan's lead. The answer is simple. The bible reveals that "All authority has been given to me (Jesus) in heaven and in earth." (Matthew 28:18) Jesus has all authority! Let's look at the word *authority*. The base of the word is AUTHOR. We know that the author of this world is not satan but God Himself. This is revealed in Genesis 1. So being that God is the giver of authority (he is the AUTHOR of all creation), and He has turned around and given all authority to Jesus, satan has no authority over you! You can claim your victory right now through this prayer:

Heavenly Father,

I come to you in Jesus name. In Your word, You have stated that all power and authority has been given to Jesus Christ. Lord I thank You for Your word and I stand on it today. Lord, I speak right now that Jesus Christ, my Lord and Savior has authority over my life. Lord, I denounce all authority that has been given to satan and his kingdom by me. I also ask You to forgive me Lord, if any of my ancestors have given it to him. I ask You God to break the ties. Help me to walk in the authority of Jesus Christ. Lord help me to follow Your word. Lord, if anything in me is operating under the false authority of satan, I plead the blood of Jesus and I ask You to renew the right spirit in me. In Jesus name I pray, amen.

Now you may have felt silly reciting those words. After all, you probably have not ever had to recite any words to operate under satan's authority. I can understand how it may seem strange. However, one has to come to the conclusion that what the bible says is the absolute truth. The bible tells us,

"For we wrestle not against flesh and blood, but against principalities, against powers, against the rulers of the darkness of this world, against spiritual wickedness in high places."(Ephesians 6:12)

Dear reader, I want you to know that there are unseen forces fighting against you. They battle you by sending you thoughts and emotions that cause you to stray from God's word. They fight against you with feelings of lust towards those things that God has forbidden us to do or even talk about. They battle you with falsehood of alternative lifestyles, pride, false gods, loneliness, depression, fear, anger and rage. In the Word of the Lord, it is stated in Ephesians 6:13-18:

Wherefore take unto you the whole armour of God, that ye may be able to withstand in the evil day, and having done all, to stand.

Stand therefore, having your loins girt about with truth, and having on the breastplate of righteousness;

And your feet shod with the preparation of the gospel of peace;

Above all, taking the shield of faith, wherewith ye shall be able to quench all the fiery darts of the wicked.

And take the helmet of salvation, and the sword of the Spirit, which is the word of God:

Praying always with all prayer and supplication in the Spirit, and watching thereunto with all perseverance and supplication for all saints;

Now this scripture is very detailed. I love the Word of God because it challenges us in ways that we may never fully understand. However, in order to get you to a place where you are able to put on the whole armour of God, I want to describe to you what each part of that scripture entails. The Bible also warns us that **"My people are destroyed for lack of knowledge." (Hosea 4:6)** This is true in every aspect of our walk with God. Many times the enemy is able to defeat us on the basis of not knowing. On that great day of judgment, I imagine many people standing before the Lord with the same reasoning "I didn't know." Although you may feel there is much about the bible and scriptures that you do not know, as a believer it is our job to find out what God is saying to His Children. We have to know how to protect ourselves and our families from every attack of the enemy. I graduated from college last year. It was a 2 year program with wonderful people who loved their profession and cared passionately about the field that they are in. They gave us a lot of work. We had assignments and deadlines as well as many different tests for each subject. Sometimes we had to do presentations. At other times,we had projects that took time and research to complete. Each time that any of that work was due, it was my responsibility to turn it in. I was expected to know enough about each subject and be ready to test when the time came. Now, it wouldn't have been smart to do but I could have waltzed into either of my many classes and not had any of the work done. Notwithstanding, when the teacher asked for the work, an answer of "I don't know" wouldn't have sufficed. My "I don't know" would have flunked me out of the program. Trust me when I tell you that satan doesn't care if you don't know. He is not going to leave you alone because the rules of his war have not been fully explained to you. We must get wisdom and with all our wisdom get an understanding of what God is saying for us to do. We must learn what we are fighting against and how to win the battle. God has equipped us with everything we need. We just need to operate in it. Let's start with the first part of this scripture and discern what it is that Paul is instructing us to do.

The first part of the Bible verse is pretty self-explanatory:

Wherefore take unto you the whole armour of God, that ye may be able to withstand in the evil day, and having done all, to stand.

This bible verse is simply reminding us that we have to put on the whole armour of God so that we can be able to withstand in the evil day. I truly believe that the 'evil day' is here and now. We live in a society plagued with all types of evil. From television, to movies, to our music, society is saturated with evil acts and thoughts of doing evil all the day long. God is admonishing us so that we can stand: stand up and say no to temptation when it comes in pulling us towards acts of sin that will separate our hearts from the Lord. Stand up and keep our faith when others are being pulled into false religions and the worship of idols instead of God. We are to stand on God's Word which promises us that He will never leave nor forsake us but will be with us even unto the end of the world. I must remind you again we are in a war. Though it be spiritual, it is as real as it gets. This is why Paul didn't say put on your clothing of God, but your ARMOUR of God. If you can begin to understand the battle, then there will be less of a hesitation when it comes to searching the Word of God to find truth. I am reminded of some of the most sobering words that Jesus has ever spoken found in Luke 13:

"Strive to enter through the narrow door. For many, I tell you, will seek to enter and will not be able."

This word was spoken about men and women of God. If we do not put on the full armour of God, if we do not stand in this evil day, we will find ourselves much like the people who are spoken about in this parable. We will be locked out. Locked out of all of the promises of God because we did not diligently seek out the Lord's will and choose to stand on His way. Dear reader, my prayer is that you will choose His way today! The next part of this scripture is:

"Stand therefore, having your loins girt about with truth, and having on the breastplate of righteousness;"

When Paul mentions the loins being girded with the "Belt of Truth" He was referring of course the Truth of God's Word. I will take it one step further and describe the truth to being Jesus Christ who is in fact the Word of God. In John 1, John describes: **"In the beginning was the Word, and the Word was with God, and the Word was God**." If you drop down further in this same book, John goes on to describe: **"And the Word was made flesh, and dwelt among us, (and we beheld his glory, the glory as of the only begotten of the Father,) full of grace and truth."** We know that a belt is fastened (or tied together) and is used to hold your armour together. Jesus Christ is the truth. He is the foundation of our faith, and our eternal hope for salvation. In John 14:6, Jesus proclaims: **"I am the way, and the truth, and the life. No one comes to the Father except through me."** Paul with his beautiful description of the belt of truth is encouraging each and everyone of us to put on the belt of truth (Jesus Christ) in order to have the protection we need to stand in evil time. We should lean on Jesus to guide us through and trust in Him to hold our armour (our protection against evil) in place. Paul described truth as having the correct information about the Lord and the Gospel of Jesus Christ. When we know our Word, when we truly know Jesus, our armour will be secure and nothing will be able to come against it. Take the time out of each day to seek God and ask Him to reveal more and more to you about His word. There are many bible apps that have great information that can help you to understand what the Bible is saying to you. Of course, nothing is as efficient as the Holy spirit who will **"teach you all things and bring all things to your remembrance."** (John 14). I must also state that the loins are a critical area to protect. As an Occupational therapy assistant I know that the lower spine controls our standing and gait pattern. If the enemy was to catch any of us not protected in that area, we could get hit and injured so badly that standing will become difficult. Also, because this is where your sexual organs are located, it will be difficult to produce fruit (of the spirit) when you are damaged in the loins.

Breastplate of Righteousness

Now I feel that it is important to note that the armour is a depiction of the Roman soldiers in the biblical times. The breastplate during the time of Romans was made from bronze and would protect the chest area. We all know that all of our organs are in this area (i.e. our heart and lungs). It is called the breastplate of righteousness (doing the ways of God). This is vitally important to do in spiritual battle because if we don't have on the righteousness of Jesus Christ, we are placing our most vital organs in danger. For example, if the enemy is looking to defeat you, and you are knowingly and freely practicing sin, it is equivalent to you having no covering over your vital organs. The enemy (who comes to kill, steal and destroy) will waste no time taking you out of the fight. This defeat would be your own fault because you didn't take the necessary steps to protect yourself. The righteousness of God is what separates us from the world. When we have good conduct, carry ourselves in holiness as God has commanded us, we are putting on that breastplate of righteousness and not allowing the enemy to defeat us.

The next verse says

And your feet shod with the preparation of the gospel of peace;

This brings to mind the bible verse Isaiah 52:7 which states:

How beautiful upon the mountains are the feet of him that bringeth good tidings, that publisheth peace; that bringeth good tidings of good, that publisheth salvation; that saith unto Zion, Thy God reigneth!

Now we should understand that our feet are to always be protected. They are our primary source of mobility. Can you imagine a soldier in an army, going to battle with all of his armour on, but no shoes? Not only would he be in danger of landmines and spikes laid by the enemy, but he/she would also be in danger of snake bites or getting severely injured by stepping on sharp rocks. It just wouldn't be a great idea. If the troop the soldier is traveling with is moving along enemy territory to attack, it would be a burden for them to have to stop or not to be able to move along as quickly because they have a soldier with compromised mobility. To have your feet shod with the preparation of the gospel is to have the word of God to move you along. You have to know it, accept it and allow it to guide you as you move along through life. You also need it when you are going through any battle in life, whether spiritual or physical. The Word of God is what we stand on. It is our foundation and our hope for the present and the future. You see in movies sometimes, soldiers marching together, with their feet totally in sync with one another. This is considered basic training for the soldiers. Soldiers are expected to maintain their dress, cover, interval, and distance. This known as DCID.

- ***Dress*** — alignment with the person to the side
- ***Cover*** — alignment with the person in front
- ***Interval*** — space between the person(s) to the side
- ***Distance*** — space between the person in front

Now if you can look at it from our experience in our Christian walk, the soldier without shoes would be compromising the *Dress* aspect right away. This in turn would change the aspect of every other part of DCID. Without shoes, the *cover* would be compromised because the person in front would possibly step on the person without shoes. The person without shoes may not even complete the cadences correctly because he/she would be so overly cautious about not being stepped on by the person in front of them. The *interval* may be off due to the fact that the soldier without shoes may be too close or too far due to the obvious compromise of their foot being stepped on. The _distance_ as well would be off. I don't know about you but I would be too cautious about injury to my feet to think about how far away I am from the person if my feet were bare. In your spiritual walk, this compromise in your covering would not allow you to move along with the march of those sharing the gospel. You wouldn't be in sync with the spirit of God which moves throughout the body of Christ. With shoes we are able to step over the most dangerous of terrains of life, with the gospel protecting us from things that would harm us greatly if our feet were uncovered. During the cold, heat, or rain, our feet would have the protection needed to move us along safely. When we are shod with the preparation of the good news of Jesus Christ (the gospel), we are prepared to go through the seasons of life without harm or injury continuing the good fight of faith till the end.

Moving on to the next part of this wonderful Word of God:

Above all, taking the shield of faith, wherewith ye shall be able to quench all the fiery darts of the wicked.

The shield is something that is definitely needed for protection. If you can picture the Roman soldier, they always had a shield. This bible verse goes on to say that your shield of faith would quench all the fiery darts of the wicked. This lets you know that it was sturdy. In Roman times, the shields that were used were huge. Sometimes, they were as large as a door. They were made of wood and then that wood would be covered in animal skin that was wet. In this way, even if the darts thrown at the soldiers were full of fire, it would be extinguished by the shield. In this same way when we as soldiers in the army of God are full of faith, we will be protected from fiery darts (situations and circumstances of life that cause us pain and anguish). Our faith in the power of God and the promises made in His Word will help us to get through those hard times which have the potential to end our walk with Christ. The bible goes on to tell us in Hebrew 11:6 that ***"without faith it is impossible to please God."*** I don't know about you , but my desire is to please the Lord. I want Him to be happy with the life that I live. You may be wondering, "How is it that I obtain faith?" We live in a world that is full of reasoning that creates doubt in the heart of believers. People will give you a thousand reasons why faith in God is hopeless and that you have to rely on the measures the world takes to be successful and have victory. I implore you to trust in the Lord. God keeps His promises. The answer to obtaining faith is more simple than you think. We must as soldiers in the army of the Lord, renew our faith through the reading of the Word of God. The Bible tells us, "Faith comes by hearing, and hearing by the Word of God." When we make a habit of studying the Word, I know it to be true that our faith will grow. You will find yourself believing all things that God has said and being strengthened even through the roughest patches in your life. The Word of God is necessary to overcome every battle and to keep you safe. I encourage you if you may be reading this and thinking, "I don't understand the Bible," to find a version of the bible that works for you. My favorite versions are the King James Version and the Amplified Version. There are also many versions available on the free bible apps that are available for all of your mobile devices. I cannot stress enough the importance of reading and studying your word. Here are some Bible verses that reveal how important this part of our armour is:

Psalm 119:105

Thy word is a lamp unto my feet, and a light unto my path.

- This reveals to us that God's Word will lead and guide us on the journey through life. Having a lamp on our feet means that we will not stumble, as God will light our way.

Proverbs 4:20-22

My son, attend to my words; incline thine ear unto my sayings. Let them not depart from thine eyes; keep them in the midst of thine heart. For they are life unto those that find them, and health to all their flesh.

- This Bible verse says that the Words of God give us life, and health. It gives us instruction to listen closely to what God is saying. I believe that not letting them depart from our eyes means to read His Word often.

2 Timothy 3:16-17

All Scripture is God-breathed and is useful for teaching, rebuking, correcting and training in righteousness, so that the servant of God may be thoroughly equipped for every good work.

- Really, I believe it speaks for itself. The Word is alive and able to help us to live pleasing to God and to train us in righteousness. It is good for us to correct ourselves and others in the faith so that we can be ready to do kingdom work!

Hebrews 4:12

For the word of God is alive and active. Sharper than any double-edged sword, it

penetrates even to dividing soul and spirit, joints and marrow; it judges the thoughts and attitudes of the heart.

- The Word may hurt, but it helps to get through fleshly desires and helps to judge our thought and heart attitudes (why we do what we do and the error or correction of our ways)

Dear reader, I pray that you have begun to feel a yearning for the word of God like never before. It is so imperative for us to fill our spirit with His truth and live according to every word of God. Only then will we be filled with the faith that is so pleasing to the heart of God and necessary to possess so that we can withstand the evil in this day.

Our next part of this scripture is two-fold:

And take the helmet of salvation, and the sword of the Spirit, which is the word of God.

Merriam Webster describes salvation as: ***deliverance from the power and effects of sin.*** To discern how this is used in our armour of protection as a helmet, we simply have to look into what a helmet does. A helmet protects your head from being injured during activities that are dangerous, such as riding a motorcycle or a bicycle. In working in a hospital for several years, I have seen first hand how much a helmet can help someone when in an accident. I have unfortunately, also seen how the lack of wearing a helmet can hinder someone when they are in an accident. One could suffer from TBI (traumatic brain injury) which can cause you to revert back to primitive instincts and rob you of your life. Adult individuals are reduced to child like behaviors and unable to learn new material. They may be unable to walk, to remember basic parts of his/her life. This person may have to have permanent caregivers to take care of them, as they may not be able to take care of themselves. It can change your life dramatically. When we view this physical truth with the spiritual eye, many of those who have not worn the helmet of salvation during spiritual battles may be left with infant like qualities that hinder their walk with Christ. One brutal attack in the Spiritual realm may hurt that individual in ways that cause them to stop in their tracks and revert to the ways of a child. Maintaining our salvation is something that we as Christians must do. Hearing the words 'maintaining in the keeping of our salvation', may seem strange. Especially when "once saved always saved" is such a popular saying. This is also an erroneous saying. Of course, to dispute the truth, we must go to the Word of God for clarity.

Matthew 24:13

But he that shall endure unto the end, the same shall be saved.

Revelation 3:5

He that overcometh, the same shall be clothed in white raiment; and I will not blot out his name from the Book of Life, but I will confess his name before My Father and before His angels.

These bible verses show us that there is a way that you can be saved and lose it. God says that He has the ability to blot out (erase) the name of an individual from the Book of Life. This is a sobering fact that should not be ignored. We definitely need to keep the helmet of salvation on so that we can be protected from being blotted out of the book of life. Our eternal abode is something that should be first priority in our life. Heaven is a prepared place for prepared people. Beloved, please do not fall into the trap of believing that your salvation is secure because of a prayer you made years ago. Salvation is truly something that we must seek and pursue everyday of our lives. We are to fill our life with prayer, praise worship, and of course self-reflection to make sure that our lives are lined up with the Word of God. Looking at it spiritually, a damaged helmet of salvation will cause us to have attacks in the mind. There will be battling of your thoughts, emotions and feelings. One of the worse feelings I have ever felt was during church services, when the Pastor or guest speaker would ask, "If you were to die today, would you make it into heaven?" I would feel so bad as the assurity of heaven as my eternal abode was a huge question in my mind. I didn't know if I would be able to make it in. This was because I been careless with my helmet of salvation. Beloved, you don't have to feel this way. You can apply your helmet of salvation and it will protect you from being unsure of your eternity. This will help you to have peace in your walk with God.

and the sword of the Spirit, which is the word of God:

This part of the scripture depicts the sword of the spirit. It is helpful that Paul revealed the Sword of the Spirit as the Word of God. The sword was the weapon used to destroy the enemy in battle. The Roman's sword and the Word of God are both described in Hebrews 4:12 which states, ***"For the word of God is alive and powerful. It is sharper than the sharpest two-edged sword, cutting between soul and spirit, between joint and marrow. It exposes our innermost thoughts and desires."***

The power of the Word of God is truly unveiled in this scripture. It is a two edged sword which means that it cuts going in and coming out. Have you ever read the scripture and it convicted your heart so badly that you had to cry out to God? That's the sheer power of the Word of God. It has the ability to take the hidden parts of our body and shed light. 2 Timothy 3:16 goes on to say that,

"All Scripture is inspired by God and is useful to teach us what is true and to make us realize what is wrong in our lives. It corrects us when we are wrong and teaches us to do what is right."

This is a sobering scripture that allows us to rest in confidence that the Bible is in fact inspired by God. We are living in a time that so many people are turned away from the Bible by people saying that the Bible is written by men and not God inspired. There are many conspiracies that convince some to stray away from the faith because they don't want to be mislead. Dear reader, please understand that all power is in God's hand. God's Word is placed on this earth to lead and guide you, and to help you in every area of your life. Don't allow anyone to tell you that scripture is not inspired by God. He is faithful to secure His Word just as He is faithful and able to secure you. Think about it for a moment. If we can believe that God created the heavens, the earth and everything in it, we must also be able to believe that He has the ability to keep His precious word written to His children protected from anyone wishing to mislead them through falsehood. All scripture is there for you and me. It is the tool that we use to defeat the enemy.

satan, our enemy, doesn't want us to know the word. This is because the Word of God has the power to defeat him. This is a truth that is displayed in the Word of God. Jesus Himself faced the enemy in the book of Luke, Chapter 4. Let's take a moment to look into this scripture:

And Jesus being full of the Holy Ghost returned from Jordan, and was led by the Spirit into the wilderness, Being forty days tempted of the devil. And in those days he did eat nothing: and when they were ended, he afterward hungered. And the devil said unto him, If thou be the Son of God, command this stone that it be made bread. And Jesus answered him, saying, <u>It is written, That man shall not live by bread alone, but by every word of God.</u> And the devil, taking him

up into an high mountain, shewed unto him all the kingdoms of the world in a moment of time.And the devil said unto him, All this power will I give thee, and the glory of them: for that is delivered unto me; and to whomsoever I will I give it. If thou therefore wilt worship me, all shall be thine. And Jesus answered and said unto him, <u>Get thee behind me, Satan: for it is written, Thou shalt worship the Lord thy God, and him only shalt thou serve.</u> And he brought him to Jerusalem, and set him on a pinnacle of the temple, and said unto him, If thou be the Son of God, cast thyself down from hence: For it is written, He shall give his angels charge over thee, to keep thee: And in their hands they shall bear thee up, lest at any time thou dash thy foot against a stone. And Jesus answering said unto him, <u>It is said, Thou shalt not tempt the Lord thy God</u>. And when the devil had ended all the temptation, he departed from him for a season.

Now I understand that this is a popular scripture. Nonetheless, I want you to really look at it with fresh eyes. Jesus was approached by satan. He wanted of course to defeat Jesus by tempting Him to go against what God called Him to do. Jesus didn't call on a thousand angels (which He could have). He didn't rebuke him in His own power (which He had the power to do). Jesus instead used all scripture to defeat satan. We look to Christ as our example of how to live. Therefore we should definitely do the same. You will notice that when Jesus used the scripture, satan went away from Him. He will depart from you as well when you use the Word of God to defeat Him. The Word of God gives us confidence when we feel down, it gives us promises when we feel all hope is gone, and joy when sadness and depression tries to overcome us. The Word of God is truly the most powerful defense we have against the forces of evil. Learn it, live it, and read it each and every day.

Chapter 21: Relationship with God

The final part of this scripture is:

Praying always with all prayer and supplication in the Spirit, and watching thereunto with all perseverance and supplication for all saints;

This scripture is instruction in actions that we should be taking, in particular, prayer. In the Muslim religion, they pray 5 times a day. These prayers are made at specific times in specified positions. Buddhists don't pray to a god but they meditate and recite mantras. Even in extreme religions (extreme being my own interpretation) such as satanism, they have prayer times. I remember seeing a video of a reformed satanist. He talked in the video of how he prayed to satan sometimes all night to gain power. This shocked me, as the last thing I associated satanism with was prayer. However, it was sobering when I compared his dedication to satan to how lukewarm I could be with my dedication towards the

Only True and Living God. I had to look at my own life and realize that my prayers were far and few in between. When I did pray, it was halfhearted and sometimes very short. I was truly ashamed. Even though I had the excuses of, "prayer is boring", and "I can't seem to focus when I pray", I felt the conviction in my heart. Beloved, prayer is one of the most powerful acts a believer can participate in. We must always pray. I remembered the bible verse Luke 18:1

"And he spake a parable unto them to this end, that men ought always to pray, and not to faint;".

Sad to say, my life was not living up to this word. To always pray sounded ridiculous to me. How could I always pray when I had to work everyday, when I had things that I did everyday that required my full attention? How could my prayers be made longer when it seemed every prayer I had prayed up until this point, had not been effective? Nevertheless, I knew that I wanted to be closer to God. So I would find time at work, when I was completely done with my patients, and had time alone, to steal away with God. I would talk to Him, telling Him how much I loved and needed Him. I took out a few pieces of paper and I wrote down my thoughts from bible passages I read, and I even wrote prayers that were evoked by the reading of the Word. God became part of my everyday routine, or should I say every night...as I would get off work at 11pm at night. I would then take a shower, turn on my gospel music, and begin a worship service with just myself and God. I did it everyday, sometimes praise dancing, sometimes singing, sometimes just crying out to God. I would belt out to Him about all of my pain, and suffering I was experiencing at the time. It was so beautiful. Soon, my prayers which were sometimes so hard to perform became a necessity for me. I HAD TO PRAY every night. This time, it wasn't because I felt forced or obligated to do it. It was so much more! Finally, I was as hungry to pray and to worship as I was for breakfast, lunch, and dinner. It didn't feel like my prayers were being sent up and falling on deaf ears (ears that refused to hear me). It was so much more. God and I had this RELATIONSHIP. This meant that both of us wanted to speak to one another all the time...it was truly a new and wonderful experience.

Chapter 22: Tarry for the Lord

Around that time, my Pastor had given His own personal testimony. He had a vision of Jesus! He talked to us about how His own personal revelation of Jesus Christ was something that had changed His life. He exhorted each and everyone of us to pray to receive our own revelation. I wanted it, badly. I listened intently to hear what he said I had to do. With such passion, and conviction in His voice, he described how he had been taught to receive the power of the Holy Spirit. He told us that we were to tarry. Merriam Webster defines tarrying as: **"to linger in expectation : WAIT 2: to abide or stay in or at a place".** He told us that we should say "Jesus, Jesus, Jesus" over and over again until the words ran together. This was such a strange description to me! He went on to say that some people of old would spend hours in God's presence just repeating the name of Jesus over and over again so that they could receive the Holy Spirit. This is how he had been able to have an experience with Jesus that was so personalized that it changed his life. Now some may think that such an encounter is very much impossible. I used to as well. However, it is important to note in 2 Corinthians 12, John stated,

"It is not expedient for me doubtless to glory. I will come to visions and revelations of the Lord. I knew a man in Christ above fourteen years ago, (whether in the body, I cannot tell; or whether out of the body, I cannot tell: God knoweth;) such an one caught up to the third heaven. And I knew such a man, (whether in the body, or out of the body, I cannot tell: God knoweth;) How that he was caught up into paradise, and heard unspeakable words, which it is not lawful for a man to utter."

This bible verse helps us to understand that there are in fact outer body experiences that happen to believers. Couple this verse with the entire book of Revelations, which is a detailed description of what is to come for sinners and believers alike. One can easily conclude that the personal experience with Christ that my Pastor was describing was quite accurately backed up with Biblical principles. These were truths that I did not know at the time. However, I was so desperate that I decided to try it, no matter how silly it sounded. So I begin, each night after I did my praise and worship (sometimes during the praise and worship) to call on the name of Jesus, Jesus, Jesus, Jesus... over and over and over again until all of my repetitions ran together like a never ending word. I will be the first to admit that it felt very strange at first. Nonetheless, I determined that it was worth the effort. I mean, to be able to say that I saw Jesus in a vision, one that was personalized just for me, was something that I was willing to feel a little silly for. So it became a habit for me. I can honestly say that in doing so, I felt such power, such a flow of peace through my body. It was something that filled me up with a desire to get closer to God and to really see Jesus face to face. It was absolutely amazing. One particular night while I was tarrying, I was on my knees near my bed. All of a sudden, I seen myself in my late grandmother's church. I was walking from the entrance of the church and I saw people all around me, very angry it seemed. My late grandmother was there, and she didn't seem happy to see me. I kept walking and I ended up towards the front of the church. Suddenly, I saw my late grandfather and he smiled at me. I gave him a hug. Now, it is very important to note that this particular grandfather I had never met. He had died long before I was born when my father was only 3 years old. That didn't create a problem spiritually, as I knew exactly who he was. I then walked towards the altar of the church and a door opened. Jesus came in. He was wearing a purple robe. His face shined. His skin was like gold. He walked towards me with open arms. I was very happy. I ended up at the front of the church with Jesus. I looked down and noticed that I was wearing an old fashioned wedding dress. This dress had a hat to match it with a veil. Jesus and I were married and Jesus ushered me out of the church. Outside was a limo. We climbed in. He looked at me. As I am writing you years later about this experience, I can still feel the love. So much love radiated from just one look, it fills my entire being to this very day! He looked at me with so much love, much more than any relationship with any man, any mother, father, sister, aunt, uncle, cousin, anybody could've have given me. Then, I noticed he searched my heart. I knew in an instant that He saw something that shouldn't be there. He then reached His hand towards the sky and the clouds opened like the door to an airplane. Light shined as it opened up and I gazed as Jesus pointed. I then came to my present sense and was still in kneeling position in my room. I was completely amazed, in awe of what God had shown me. I was in complete wonderment of what it was that had just transpired in my tarrying. From that moment on, I begin to understand that Jesus's love for me was absolutely above and beyond my comprehension. The fact that I wore a bridal gown in my vision represented I was part of His church, His bride that is talked about in Revelations 19:7, which states:

> ***Let us be glad and rejoice, and give honour to Him: for the marriage of the Lamb is come, and his wife hath made herself ready. And to her was granted that she should be arrayed in fine linen, clean and white: for the fine linen is the righteousness of saints.***

This was God's way of personalizing my revelation of who He is and what purpose He has for me in life. It truly has changed my outlook on the future and heightened my passion for eternity. The love that has been revealed with just one look at me still reverberates in my soul. Are you experiencing visions such as this in your prayer life? This type of experience is not reserved for ministers and prophets. God desires every one of His children to experience his/her own vision and encounter with Christ. There have been many other times that I tarry and it's like I am operating in two forms of self. With my mouth, my spirit is saying Jesus, Jesus, Jesus, Jesus, over and over again until I speak in unknown languages (which some call speaking in tongues). It is amazing, many times it's as if my voice and spirit are speaking in one conversation with God, and in my mind, I am unable to discern what my mouth is speaking. This has been something that confounded me until I spoke with my brother about it. He revealed that the Holy Spirit will make intercession for you. My mouth and my spirit were the tools that the Holy spirit utilized to intercede for me. This is a truth revealed in Romans 8:26 which states,

"And the Holy Spirit helps us in our weakness. For example, we don't know what God wants us to pray for. But the Holy Spirit prays for us with groanings that cannot be expressed in words."

I can be perfectly honest in saying that for a very long time I felt that prayer was boring, that it was a chore to do. Amazingly, after my experience with Jesus, and as the Holy Spirit continued to intercede for me, it became different. No longer was I forcing myself to perform prayer and worship time, but I was yearning for it. I found myself racing home so I could get the time in with the Lord. I was in a place of passion and pursuit of something that was so exciting and new. It was better than a new relationship. It was better than anything. As I grew in the Spirit, it became normal for me to wake up, 3 o'clock in the morning to pray and to fellowship with the Lord. God truly became my best friend. The more time I spent with Him, the more I was able to truly see myself for who I was. Although I considered myself to be normal and happy, there was so much hidden pain that I had deep inside of me, that I literally would find myself crying and crying to the Lord. I can feel God even now. A prayerful relationship with the Father involves us really being able to uncover years of hidden pain and suffering. Beloved He wants to heal you! His desire is for you to be set free from everything that has held you in bondage. No matter what it is that you have been going through, there is power and strength in developing a prayerful life. It is pivotal to our growth in Him. As we are speaking on this subject, I want to know how often you take the time to be vulnerable with the Lord. It's okay to be perfectly honest. We as humans in this society that promotes independence sometimes find it very hard to allow even God to see our flaws. Somehow we think that in order to have God in our life, we need to get ourselves together. Then, we say, we will be able to really enjoy our relationship with Him. That would easily be equivocated to not going to the hospital until you feel better. The hospital was created to treat the sick. God desires to make you whole and you cannot do it by yourself, no matter how hard you try. When I was beginning my walk with the Lord, I remember I had a habit of smoking a cigar and drinking alcohol every day. I believe that in my mind I justified it as a sleep aid. When I begin going to church, nothing changed. I would still come home and smoke my cigar and drink. I ended up spending more time at the church and even getting involved in small study groups. This created a great conviction in me because I knew the habits were contrary to the Word of God. I felt that it was my obligation to end this love and practice of smoking and drinking. I was determined to get myself right so that God could fully use me. It became a habit for me to go to the altar every time my Pastor did an altar call. I would go up to the altar, pray earnestly for God to take away my smoking and drinking habit, then I would get home and do the same thing. This in turn would make me ashamed and angry with myself, and more determined to go to the altar, ask God to change me, and start all over again. Romans 7:14-23 states,

> *"We know that the law is spiritual; but I am unspiritual, sold as a slave to sin. I do not understand what I do. For what I want to do I do not do, but what I hate I do. And if I do what I do not want to do, I agree that the law is good. As it is, it is no longer I myself who do it, but it is sin living in me. For I know that good itself does not dwell in me, that is, in my sinful nature. For I have the desire to do what is good, but I cannot carry it out. For I do not do the good I want to do, but the evil I do not want to do—this I keep*

on doing. Now if I do what I do not want to do, it is no longer I who do it, but it is sin living in me that does it. So I find this law at work: Although I want to do good, evil is right there with me. For in my inner being I delight in God's law; but I see another law at work in me, waging war against the law of my mind and making me a prisoner of the law of sin at work within me."

I was indeed a slave to sin. There was so much inside of me that I didn't understand. I found myself just like Paul in this scripture. I was truly doing exactly what I didn't want to do. I hated the fact that I was so wrapped up in this sin and I knew that it went against the Word of God. My body is God's temple. I was destroying it with poisons that were designed to kill me. I was frustrated even the more because as much as I desired to stop smoking, I kept doing it. As much as I wanted to stop drinking, I just kept drinking...in spite of myself. This created embarrassment and depression. I felt like a failure. Perhaps you feel the same way with some sin that is frustrating you. If you are in a place like this in your life, whether it be sexual immorality, drug addiction, anger, depression, whatever your sin may be, God is able to help you! I am a living witness. I remember finally getting to to the point that I felt, I CAN'T DO

THIS! I was so disgusted with how many times I had made empty promises and false proclamations that I was going to quit my habits and then fall right into the trap of performing those same sins over and over again. I was tired of going up to the altar every Sunday, hoping that God would change me, and then getting home and returning to my sins. I called myself angry with God and frustrated to the point that this was the end of my ropes. As Pastor summoned for the altar call that following Sunday, I went up to the front of the church with determination in my heart. I was going to give God a piece of my mind. They had told me that He desires for us to be real with Him and that was exactly what I was about to do. I walked right up to the front of the church and I told God in my most unfiltered way, "Lord, I am a smoker. I drink, and I do it everyday. I have repented to you, and still have been unable to stop myself. If you want me to stop, YOU are going to have to do it for me. I am not able to do this." I don't honestly remember a great moment that happened to confirm whether this conclusion was a grand thing in God's eyes. Pastor didn't proclaim to me that God had even honored my prayer. He had no idea what I prayed about because this conversation was between God and I. I went back to my seat and that was that. When I got home, I remember that night, setting out my cigar and my alcohol and watching t.v. I had the undeniable urge to smoke and drink and I was going to, but I wanted to watch my favorite television shows first. When I woke up, it was the next morning. Undoubtedly, the cigar and alcohol was sitting where I had left it, and I put it away. The next evening, I said to myself, "This is going to be the night that I finish that alcohol and smoke my cigar." I sat in the living room and I was as determined as I was the night before to finish watching my shows so that I could smoke and drink after. I woke up, again it was morning so I just put my drink back in the fridge and headed out. This went on for a few days and by the 4th night, I said to myself "I am going to smoke and drink. I will not go back to sleep." So here I was, lighting my cigar to watch television and took a nice long drag off of it. Oh! It truly tasted like tar! I begin to look at the box and the cigar (thinking it was just a bad tasting cigar). The same was true for my drink. I did not care for the taste. I was puzzled, as we sometimes are, even though we are "believers". I didn't understand why the taste was taken from me. Sometime later, the Holy Spirit revealed that God had taken the taste out of my mouth. I am very happy to say that I never went back to my nightly ritual. It was just something that God had wiped away from me. I am now more than ever convinced that no matter how much I detested what I was doing, without the help of Jesus Christ, I would have continued in sin. This is because the truth of the matter is, we can do nothing without Him. I had been deceived into thinking that once I made up my mind about sin, I could overcome it on my own. I believed in my heart that empty declarations made at the altar would create a change necessary in my life to live according to the law of God. This may be something that you have been taught as well, as it is common with believers. Many of us live our entire lives trying with all our might to do God's will because we believe that Jesus is the Son of God. We trust that if we do His will, we will be able to destroy sin and turn a deaf ear to temptation. Then as we fail Him over and over again, we feel helpless to sin, and often arrive to the point where we just allow it to overtake us when it comes. Many of us have spent years thinking that we are just unable to be free from the bondages that life brings our way. Beloved, this is a lie from the enemy. The Word of God reveals that all have sinned, and fallen short of the glory of God. Sin is the sickness that we are born with. We are helpless to it, and without the help of a risen Savior, we will die in it. Knowing the Word of God alone is not going to help you to be free from it. Attending every church service held in your ministry is not going to let you escape it. No amount of charitable deeds will free you from its grasp. We really err in our ways when we try to align our ways with God's ways without Him. Besides, Isaiah 64:6 reveals to us that

"We are all infected and impure with sin. When we display our righteous deeds, they are nothing but filthy rags. Like autumn leaves, we wither and fall, and our sins sweep us away like the wind."

Chapter 23: Lord, How Deeply We Need You

If we didn't need Jesus to help us to be free, then He never would have died on the cross. It is really an act of arrogance when we attempt to fix ourselves without the sacrifice He made for us. Imagine someone in need of surgery on their legs, due to an injury that has prevented them from walking. The doctor has given them written instructions on how they are desperately in need of a specialized physician who is able to go into their legs and operate so that they will be able to walk again. This person gets very excited at hearing this! They are thankful to the surgeon for helping them to realize that the need for surgery is there. However, instead of going to the surgeon to receive the necessary procedure that they need for their leg, they try on their own to fix the problem. They look at the manual and learn all that need to know about how a person can be able to walk and they attempt to do it themselves. This, of course, would cause even more damage and discourage the potential patient from even going to the doctor because their false sense of superiority has been damaged. Their failed attempt now makes them believe that they are unworthy of going to the surgeon, and if they have tried and been unsuccessful in their trying, then why even keep trying. It sounds ridiculous but this is what we do each and every time we try to "fix what's wrong with us" apart from God.

I truly believe that this what Jesus was speaking about when He gave the wedding banquet parable in Matthew 22...

And Jesus answered and spake unto them again by parables, and said, The kingdom of heaven is like unto a certain king, which made a marriage for his son, And sent forth his servants to call them that were bidden to the wedding: and they would not come.Again, he sent forth other servants, saying, Tell them which are bidden, Behold, I have prepared my dinner: my oxen and my fatlings are killed, and all things are ready: come unto the marriage. But they made light of it, and went their ways, one to his farm, another to his merchandise: And the remnant took his servants, and entreated them spitefully, and slew them. But when the king heard thereof, he was wroth: and he sent forth his armies, and destroyed those murderers, and burned up their city. Then saith he to his servants, The wedding is ready, but they which were bidden were not worthy. Go ye therefore into the highways, and as many as ye shall find, bid to the marriage. So those servants went out into the highways, and gathered together all as many as they found, both bad and good: and the wedding was furnished with guests. And when the king came in to see the guests, he saw there a man which had not on a wedding garment: And he saith unto him, Friend, how camest thou in hither not having a wedding garment? And he was speechless. Then said the king to the servants, Bind him hand and foot, and take him away, and cast him into outer darkness, there shall be weeping and gnashing of teeth. For many are called, but few are chosen.

This servant had the invite to the wedding. We can use context clues to come to the conclusion that the wedding garments have been provided to the individual. However, because of pride, or simple ignorance, this servant came with his own clothes that were unacceptable to God. This is our righteousness, our "fixing" of what is wrong with us outside of God. The blood Jesus shed on the cross was for the remission of sins. Remission is **the cancellation of a debt, charge, or penalty.** Follow me now. Romans 6:23 reminds of what debt has been paid off.

For the wages of sin is death, but the free gift of God is eternal life through Christ Jesus our Lord.

Jesus paid a price for us. The penalty for sin is death. Rightfully because we are born into sin and live and battle with sin all of our lives, we were sentenced to death. However, God in all of His love and compassion for us, sent His only begotten Son to die for us and to help us to have a path back to reconciliation with the Father. The only way that we can get on that path is through Jesus Christ. He is our guide back to the path of righteousness. Comparing this to the parable about the servant with the garment, I believe that the garment represents the righteousness of Jesus Christ. No amount of good deeds will allow us to surpass what He has already done in His life being laid down to pay our penalty. His righteousness is given freely to us when we accept Him as our Lord and Savior. This can become a familiar concept that leads people into error as they take lightly the position Jesus is in, presiding as our Lord. This word Lord is defined as **someone or something having power, authority, or influence; a master or ruler.** When you accept Jesus as Lord, you are saying that He fits that definition in your life. You are allowing Him to have power, authority, and influence in your life. You are deeming Him as master or ruler of your life. I ask you to think about that for a moment. I believe that many people tend to overlook what this entails. Power means **the ability to do something or act in a**

particular way, especially as a faculty or quality. Let's recognize that in placing Jesus as Lord over your life, you are submitting your power to Him. He makes the rules. For example, the world says "It's okay for you to date someone and have casual sexual encounters." As a Christian, you have said that Jesus is the Lord over your life. Therefore, the power to do as the world does is no longer up for your choosing. The power is given to Him and He says that we should not fornicate. As a matter of fact, the bible clearly states in 1 Corinthians 6:18:

Flee from sexual immorality. Every other sin a person commits is outside the body, but the sexually immoral person sins against his own body.

Sexual immorality is not just fornication, but is an umbrella term for any sexual acts performed outside of marriage such as fornication, adultry, homosexuality, pornongraphy, etc. I know in my own life, this was not something that was taught to me. I knew PLENTY of people in the church who had live in spouses whom they were NOT married to, or even engaged in sexual activity with many different people in different seasons of their lives. There were even some who were married and were committing adultery with people inside the church. Many people were homosexual and people knew it, but did not remind the individuals about the word of God which calls such acts abominations. Beloved, this goes against God's word. God states that we should not participate in sexual immorality, and being that we as believers (true believers) of God's Word have given Jesus power over us, we must allow Him to be Lord and exercise His power.

The next part of Jesus being Lord over our life is us giving Him **authority** over our lives. Google defines authority as: *the power or right to give orders, make decisions, and enforce obedience.* So, let's look into another example to see what it it is to truly give Jesus the authority (which is a branch of having power) over our life. The Bible in Ephesians 4:31-32:

Get rid of all bitterness, rage, anger, harsh words, and slander, as well as all types of evil behavior. Instead, be kind to each other, tenderhearted, forgiving one another, just as God through Christ has forgiven you.

I don't think that the Bible could've been any clearer in letting us know what Christ expects out of us. In the world we are told that "revenge is sweet". We are also told even as children that we are able to say a few angry words when we are mad. We see reality shows and movies that glorify people speaking harsh words and slandering the names of one another when they are in disagreement. I have often met Christians who for whatever reason have come to a point of disagreement and they end up arguing, not speaking, and saying very mean things to each other and to others about one another. This should not be so, love. As Lord over our life, Jesus has made it apparent that we should put away bitterness, anger, rage, harsh words, slander and evil behavior. If we have truly given Him authority that comes with Lordship over our lives, we don't even have the right to make a decision to be angry to the point of using harsh words, slander, or harboring bitterness towards ANYONE. Do you understand the weight of that? The role of being Lord over our lives gives Jesus the power of making the decision for us in the realm of how to react to a situation! I have 2 children who I love dearly. I set standards high for them and they sometimes have lots of household chores, long days of homework, prayer and studying. I know it can be frustrating for them. Yet as a parent, I don't allow room for attitudes with me. Even if they are at a point of anger or resentment for the responsibilities they have at any given time, they are expected to accept their role as good children and be obedient and control their anger. Angry outbursts are not tolerated. My parents expected the same out of me. It was a hard pill to swallow. As an adult, one may easily feel that NOBODY has the right to tell us whether or not we should respond with harsh words when someone has made us angry. I definitely felt for a long time that no one could tell me not to hold bitterness towards another person when they did me wrong. Even the thought of someone telling me that I shouldn't be mad sounded absurd to me. Nevertheless, the act of making Jesus Christ my Lord and Savior placed me in that situation. In order for me to truly be His follower and Him to be my Lord, He deserved the right to tell me exactly what I should do in any situation. I didn't know that for many years. I would fight, sometimes even physically, when I felt that someone had wronged me. I would hold bitterness in my heart when people hurt me, especially when I didn't deserve it (in my opinion). Are you feeling the same way? In our society the idea of not having a "God-given" gift of choice in how we react to situations that directly affect us seems silly and unbelievable. Even the most devout Christians are expected to have at least an outburst of anger from time to time, as they are only human and people do a lot of things against them sometimes purposely. However, in the kingdom of God, it is not a democracy. We don't pick and choose which parts we follow and which parts we feel are fair or which parts seem to be realistic according to our own reasoning. The act of making Jesus our Lord eliminates every right to go against it in any way.

The next part of the Lordship of Jesus Christ is influence. Influence defined in Google is: ***the capacity to have an effect on the character, development, or behavior of someone or something, or the effect itself.*** This is powerful! The act of Jesus Christ being your Lord includes Him having an effect on you character, how you develop and even your behavior! What type of behavior and character? Well the behavior that Christ exhibited while He was on this Earth. I have this personal theory that everyone you spend time with has the power to influence you in one way or another. This has been particularly true in my own personal life. I remember being in my mid 20s (I am aging myself) and I truly hated the camera. I hated being in front of it, unless we were in a photo studio. I met some young ladies that really loved the camera. Every time they had the opportunity to get in front of the camera, they were ready. It really was different to me because I had never been that way. Nevertheless, they influenced me greatly. I begin going home and posing for the cameras. I even learned how to upload photos to sites that had emojis and cute words that could be added to make the photos even more beautiful. It gave me a boost in confidence, and helped me to become more comfortable with pictures. I've also had people to influence me in how I dress, phrases that I use, and hairstyles. Most of all,

I have been taught in the church by other believers the principles of having a good prayer life, how to make reading the word a part of my everyday life, and how to encourage others in Christ. These are principles that have the power to influence others as well. I have met many people who have noticed my encouraging and loving nature and complimenting me on it. I give all glory to God. Before giving my life to Jesus, I was mean and would spew out harsh words towards people with no reason. I was very vindictive and angry with the world. When I tell people who I know now about that time in my life, they find it unbelievable. Truly it was Christ that changed me. In all of my prayer time, reading the word, and fellowshipping with other believers, the love of Christ overtook me. I found myself being full of compassion and leaning on Christ when people wronged me. Jesus Christ's influence is a beautiful covering that takes place in your life and changes your world. Love becomes a part of who you are. You talk differently, you think differently, your motives are changed. Perhaps this is why the Bible states,

John 13:35
By this shall all men know that ye are my disciples, if ye have love one to another.

Romans 12:2

Don't copy the behavior and customs of this world, but let God transform you into a new person by changing the way you think. Then you will learn to know God's will for you, which is good and pleasing and perfect.

1 Peter 4:1-2
Therefore, since Christ has suffered in the flesh, arm yourselves also with the same purpose, because he who has suffered in the flesh has ceased from sin, so as to live the rest of the time in the flesh no longer for the lusts of men, but for the will of God.

John 14:12
"I tell you the truth, anyone who believes in me will do the same works I have done, and even greater works, because I am going to be with the Father.

These bible verses clearly reveal a pattern of the believer who denies the influence of the world and allows the influence of Christ to lead and guide him/her into all truths. This is a way of life that sounds simple, but can prove to be quite difficult. The influence that things like culture, popular beliefs, peer circles, and media have on an individual can be overwhelming, to say the least. I would like to say that it is reserved for teens and young adults but the older I get, the more I realize that the pressure is present at every age and in every walk of life. The world bombards you with its own opinion of what type of parent you should be, how you should dress, what type of job you should work, car you should drive and house you should live in. It's very challenging to not fall into the habit of doing what everyone else feels is appropriate in various areas of our lives. Society has an "acceptable" behavior, dress, talk, and even life choice pattern. We are told either directly or given demonstration through avenues like television and popular theories on what we should be focusing on, and things that we need to be concerned about dependent upon our age, gender, or culture. Even the very ministries that we are involved in, if we are not too careful, can lead us astray into following customs and traditions that do not glorify God in the least. We have to keep that connection with God and surrender our own belief system of what we should be focusing on, what our behaviors should entail, how we live our lives in general when it comes to allowing Jesus to reign in our lives. I know that it is not easy. What simplifies it for me is what the Word of God says about those who choose to follow the world instead of God. The bible reveals how different the influence of God is compared to the world:

James 4:4

You adulterous people, don't you know that friendship with the world means enmity against God? Therefore, anyone who chooses to be a friend of the world becomes an enemy of God.

When Jesus becomes your Lord, the Holy Spirit will come into you and teach you all things about Christ. He will lead you and guide you into the influence of Christ. Naturally, you will hate the things of the world. Friendship with the world is a dangerous thing because you are made to be the enemy of God. When I hear the words "enemy of God" I think of satan and people who worship satan. Maybe even those who are mean, hateful and murdering Christians, or killing children, or burning down churches in their direct hate for God. However, this Bible verse is not talking about those extreme circumstances. This is about simply loving the things of the world. You have met people that may love the things of this world, like money, power, fame, and fortune. These are people that probably don't even consider eternity when they factor in the many plans that they have made for their life. It is an easy trap to get into because the people who are unsaved and saved alike have goals, plans, visions and dreams that they work hard to fulfill. If we aren't careful, these goals visions and dreams that are centered around ourselves and the things that this world has to offer will cause us to become lovers of this world. I have learned that when you are chosen by God, it causes you to be rejected by the world. Even as a child, I was the one that everyone picked on and talked about. We lived a hard life. Sometimes we had no running water, no electricity. We went to school stink and dirty because of living conditions at home. This rejection could have caused me to long for beautiful clothes, and to have the admiration of this world instead of the hate that I had received as a child. I thank God for Jesus. He came in and caused me to long for Him during the times that I felt alone. Many of us do not have that opportunity though. Sometimes we feel so rejected by the world that it makes us want to feel accepted by it more. So we can become like the world, determined to get the things that we didn't have and to have even more than everyone else so that they can admire us. You see this trait in many celebrities lives who are constantly seeking the world's approval. Can I tell you a secret? They will never truly approve. We can spend our entire lives changing our looks, buying more and more flashy clothes, making sure that our hair, jewelry, and cars that we drive are all top of the line and at the end of the day, somebody somewhere will find something wrong with you. More importantly, even if you do somehow get to the world's most admired status, and all the world loves you, what have you really gained? The bible says that you have made friendship with the world, which places you as the enemy of God. I don't know about you, but to me that sounds like a scary place to be. In looking up exactly what the fate of God's enemies are, one is able to understand the true price of falling in love with the world and making friendship with it:

Nahum 1:2

A jealous and avenging God is the LORD; The LORD is avenging and wrathful The LORD takes vengeance on His adversaries, And He reserves wrath for His enemies.

Judges 5:31

"Thus let all Your enemies perish, O LORD; But let those who love Him be like the rising of the sun in its might." ...

Psalms 92:9

For, behold, Your enemies, O LORD, For, behold, Your enemies will perish; All who do iniquity will be scattered.

Prior to me being able to fully understand that friendship with the world places us as enemies of God, these bible verses about the fate of God's enemies seemed very justified. Obviously those "baby killing Christian hating church burners" deserved to be destroyed by the God they hated. It is a sobering truth when you realize how easily one can be led into the position of being God's enemy. Dear reader, please understand that God loves you very much and nothing that this world has to offer will ever compare to all that God has planned for those that love Him. If you are reading this and have realized that in some area of your life, you have fallen in love with things of the world, it is not too late. God has made a way out. Cling to Him and be delivered from whatever causes you to seek outside of God for happiness, joy, and peace that only God truly has to offer you. Some of the saddest people in the world have everything that we think will make us happy. Often I hear of stories about stars that I love to watch, and music stars that I loved to hear sing or rap committing suicide. You wonder how these people could possibly feel so bad about themselves when the world adores them but the answer is simple. Life without Jesus Christ is like being a fish with no water, or a plant with no sun. You cannot get the life giving power that we need to survive. I thank God that He created us in His image and likeness, and placed a desire in our hearts to have a relationship with Him.

Chapter 24: Making Jesus our Master and Ruler

The final part of making Jesus Christ our Lord is giving place for Him to be your master or ruler. Let's define these 2 terms.

Master: a person who has people working for him, especially servants or slaves.

Ruler: a person exercising government or dominion.

These two terms are very closely related. They can almost be interchangeable. Being that Jesus is being placed in a place of our lives speaks volumes. We know that slaves have little to no rights outside of what his/her master gives. Can you imagine during slavery times a master telling his/her slave to do something and the slave saying to them "I don't think that is right," or refusing to even acknowledge the orders that the master has given? The consequences are unmentionable but we do it to God everyday. He has told us to "love our neighbor" and some of us are fighting, cursing and hating our neighbors, yet still claiming Jesus as our Lord. He has instructed husbands to "love their wives as Christ loved the church." However, men are cheating on their wives, belittling their feelings, talking harsh to them and even raising hands to hit their wives behind closed doors. Some of these people are still claiming Christ as their Lord. Children are told to obey their parents in the Lord, yet you see talk shows and sadly even news stories where children are rebelling, cursing,fighting and even killing their parents. I believe if you talk to those same disobedient children, they will claim Jesus as their Lord. If Jesus was in fact our master, which would deem us as slaves to His commands, there would be no room to go against His commandments. If He was in fact able to exercise dominion the way that the definition of Lord entails, we should not be so far from who Jesus was. Every law and commandment points us back to His character. He is everything that the Word commands us to be. I remember hearing a story about Abraham Lincoln in his years prior to becoming the president of the United States. He had never been to a slave auction and decided one day that He would go. When he went, he saw a young black woman who was being auctioned off. Many men were around in a bidding war, hoping to get this young beautiful slave woman because becoming her master meant that she had to do whatever they wanted her to do. Keep in mind that it was no secret that many of the slave owners of that time used the women for sex whenever they pleased. I am sure many of them had all kinds of filthy pleasure seeking motives behind their bidding. Abraham Lincoln decided to enter the bidding himself. After a few rounds of the price going higher and higher, he won the bid for this beautiful black slave. She was of course, frightened and helpless to do whatever he wanted of her as her new master. However, Abraham Lincoln had different plans for this slave. He looked at her and told her that she was free. Freedom at that time had not been given to the slaves (as it was Abraham Lincoln later as president who would declare them all free.) Frightened, the young lady informed the future president that she didn't understand what He meant by saying that she was free. Abraham then explained to her that she was free to do whatever she wanted and go wherever she wanted to go. The young lady told him, "Well I will go with you." This story reflects what it means when we deem Jesus as our Lord (master, ruler) in our life. He has set us free from the bondage of sin. In return we should be happy to go with Him, walk with Him, do what He wants us to do. That means absolutely every word of the bible, as it is written instruction from the spirit of God to instruct and equip us with the wisdom we need to be who God created us to be.

So let's put it all together. Jesus as Lord looks very different than what most people envision it, or even in vast contrast to how most Christians live. Is

He able to make decisions for you? Does He influence how you think to the point that you are unable to act the way that our flesh desires? Is he the authoritative figure in your life? These are the things that we have to consider before we decide to even accept Christ. He is freely your Savior (it was His pleasure to die for everyone's sin), it is our choice to whether He is our Lord. I have met many people that like to "cherry pick" scriptures. They find some parts of the bible that they want to follow wholeheartedly and other parts that they do not want to even try to discuss. Being a Christian who frequently interacts heavily with other believers on social media sites, I get asked constantly questions like "Do you believe in the Old Testament?". To me, it's crazy to think of the old and new testaments as two separate beliefs. However, you will find people who proclaim Jesus as Lord, but only believe certain truths about the bible and other truths they simply choose not to follow. I had a person of a different faith come to my house one day. I answered the door, curious to know what word she would like to share with me. She spoke many truths, but when it came to the truth of Jesus Christ being the Son of God, she disagreed with me. She told me that she believes that Jesus exists, but that he was just a prophet, not part of the trinity. In fact, she told me that the trinity doesn't even exist. This really broke my heart to hear, as I realized the falsehood that she sadly believed as truth. It would definitely be a sure trap in the end. For this falsehood held the power of making her miss her open invitation to an eternity in heaven with God the Father, God the Son and God the Holy Spirit. It is important to know that God gives us free will. He wants us to choose Him but will not force Himself upon us. Needless to say, He is a Holy God. Following Him is not a mystical term that has many meanings but only one meaning. We as children played a 'follow the leader' game that my cousins taught me as a child, Punchinello funny fellow. In this game we asked "What can you do Punchinello funny fellow?". This was the time for whomever was playing the role as 'Punchinello' to do a dance or strike a pose. Our reply after the person did their dance or their pose was to say to him/her "We can do it too Punchinello Funny Fellow", and then we mimicked or imitated the exact move or pose the person did prior. I smile thinking about how funny and silly that little game was but the rules were simple. Whatever that person who was playing the role of Punchinello (my spell check is lighting up red) did, we followed. Strangely enough, we don't do that with Jesus. We say, "Well, He did this, but I don't want to do that." or "The Bible says this, but I don't believe it." St Augustine had a great saying about this type of situation. ***"If you believe in the Gospel what you like, and reject what you don't like,*** *it is not the Gospel you believe, but yourself."* When you look at picking the scriptures out to weigh in your opinion about whether you believe what they say or if you should follow them, you are believing only in yourself. This in truth is why so many people have different religious beliefs but will quickly claim that they are all serving the same God. Jesus said Himself, in Luke 6:46*"So why do you keep calling me 'Lord, Lord!' when you don't do what I say?"* It is only lip service, and is not profitable at all in the Kingdom of Heaven. We live in a society full of people who are accustomed to living a lie. Social media sites are full of moms who have plenty of pictures of their children that they don't take care of. Dads post pictures of money and then claim bankruptcy when they are in child support court. Best friends take pictures together and claim to be "sisters" but talk so badly behind each others back that it is shameful. People who are chronic cheaters will fill their pages up with pictures of his/her spouse and have affairs in real life everyday. We watched staged reality shows and operate in churches who claim to be for the Lord but are secretly only looking out for the best interest of select "top givers" and the family of the leaders. It's easy to become so blended with the lies that are lived that one never takes the time to weigh out if he/she is truly allowing Jesus to reign as Lord in their life. Beloved, don't fall into that trap.... this is vitally important! Remember the bible verse when people were standing before Jesus stating all the good that they have done in prophesying, performing miracles and even casting out devils in Jesus name. Sadly, He told them, "I never knew you." Those words resonate in my heart and cause such a sadness in my spirit that I am welling with tears as I type this to you. Judgment day is the final day. There will be no do overs. There will be no way for you to turn around your life and do better. The time is truly now for salvation.

After reading this, you may feel that you need to evaluate whether Jesus is the Lord of your life. I truly pray that you are. The only way that we will ever be able to face God with the confidence in our walk is if we have completely surrendered to Christ and allowed Him to reign as our Savior.

Chapter 25: God .Rage. Eternity and YOU

We could learn a lot about judgment day when we examine the life of Rage. By 'we' I mean you and I. Writing this book has opened my eyes to so many truths as I know that truly the Lord had a hand in the process. While Raegina may be a fictional character, in truth she represents many of us - as we all have a day where we will indeed face the True and Living God. Many of her habits and behaviors exhibited are those that the everyday Christian faces. We all have things about us that need some type of deliverance. I know this because the bible tells us plainly:

What then? are we better than they? No, in no wise: for we have before proved both Jews and Gentiles, that they are all under sin;

As it is written, There is none righteous, no, not one:

Romans 3:9-10

Even the greatest ministers, the best praise dancers, the most prestigious missionaries, evangelists and priests have sinned and are in need of deliverance. No one is exempt. Therefore, it would be wise for each of us to examine our hearts and minds to be sure of what God is expecting, and what we are lacking. It is the only way that we can be sure of our standing with the Lord. How tragic would it be to read and understand the contents of this book, and not apply the knowledge to our lives. Heaven is a prepared place for prepared people. Let's look into the life of Rage.

Sexual Immorality

Let's just start with the most obvious sin that Rage was deeply engrossed in. She was involved in a sexual relationship with a man who was not her husband. This is what the bible calls fornication. Many of us have been in or may currently be in a relationship with a boyfriend, girlfriend, or even someone who we have no official title with, sexually. Beloved, this in God's eyes, is a sin. The bible tells us In 1 Corinthians 6:18 that we should:

Run from sexual sin! No other sin so clearly affects the body as this one does. For sexual immorality is a sin against your own body.

This truth is sobering. To be honest, I have read this verse many times, but it took the Holy Spirit to help me to understand the severity of what Paul was saying in it. Many people laugh at me about this, but

I am overly cautious when it comes to unfamiliar surroundings. I have heard too many stories of people who went to certain cities and ended up robbed, hurt, or even killed. Therefore, I roll my windows up and avoid neighborhoods that look questionable. We live in a crazy world. Let's pretend that upon arriving in the new city, for whichever reason, you ask a friend about the city. It is called "Fornication". Upon hearing this city's name your friend tells you to run!!! How would that make you feel? Would you just ignore the warning and find a hotel in the city of Fornication? Would you go into the city and trust that it is safe anyway? I hope not! The fact that your friend has told you that you should run from this city should be evidence enough that this place is not somewhere you should be. Nonetheless we, (myself included) are easy to fall into the worldly ways of casual sex with whomever we find ourselves sexually attracted to. You may have a reason behind why you are involved in a relationship that involves this sin, and I understand. All 3 of my past relationships have been in this category at one point or another. You "plan on getting married", or you "feel like the sexual sin is the only one that you are committing" so you don't try to abstain from it. Listen and trust me when I tell you that this is a grave error.

If you pay attention to what this bible verse is telling us, the sin of sexual immorality is unique in that it is the only sin that one commits in which he/she is sinning within himself/herself. We know that the bible also reminds us in the very next verses: ***Or do you not know that your body is the temple of the Holy Spirit who is in you, whom you have from God, and you are not your own? For you were bought at a price; therefore glorify God in your body and in your spirit, which are God's.***

This powerful scripture lets us know that once we accept Jesus Christ as our Savior, we are not our own, we are bought with a price. This is a revelation that many Christians have not yet comprehended. We believe that salvation is some type of instantaneous act that eliminates the possibility of consequence of sin for our actions, as long as we repent and confess our sins. I remember that after the demise of my marriage, I was saved and delivered. I met someone who I thought was "the one" and I made it very clear that I would not be engaging in sexual acts. I wanted to wait until marriage. So, in the beginning, I did really well. I didn't even kiss him because I didn't want to be involved in any questionable activity. That idea lasted for a while, but eventually, I felt that I was being "too saved" and that it would be okay for a hug, a kiss, and maybe even cuddling, as long as I didn't cross that line. This was arrogance at it's best. The audacity of me to think that somehow my "human will" was enough to help me to not sin against God with sexual acts. Eventually I gave way and ended up having sex with him. I will never forget the night that we decided to commit this sinful act, well I decided, as it was already in his heart. I could feel the Holy Spirit inside of me crying out for me not to commit this act. My own reasoning of "well, it's not a huge sin" and "God will forgive me" was the loudest voice and of course overtook that weak "human will" to stay pure before God. As the decision was made on my part, a tear fell from my eye. I knew that it was the Holy Spirit removing His presence from me. It still hurts my heart today that I was so careless in what I had done. The Holy Spirit is my friend. He is my confidant. He is my comforter, there for me when nobody else is, petitioning the Father on my behalf, pulling me into God's presence with His power. He changed my life from darkness to light. My body is the temple of the Holy Spirit. It is where He lives. Beloved, when we engage in sinful sexual acts, we are forcing the Holy Spirit out and welcoming the enemy in. To put it more bluntly if I may, engaging in sexual acts with the indwelling of the Holy Spirit would be equivalent to you asking the Holy Spirit to participate or engage in the sexual act with you. It sounds perverse, because it is in fact perverse. We cannot expect to flourish in the Spirit of the Living God when we are allowing such evil and perverse spirits to live within us. We must do as Paul has directed us and flee sexual immorality.

I found that once I had engaged in the sexual acts, it was like a drug, I wanted more, and the more I engaged in them, the less the Word of God about that particular sin penetrated my heart. I was trapped. Many of you may be feeling trapped right now in sexual immorality, whether it be: fornication, adultery, homosexuality, masturbation, or any other sexual sin. There is freedom found in Jesus Christ. We have to count the costs. Think about it like this: is whatever sin it is that you are involved in worth your eternity? Is it worth kicking out the precious Holy Spirit to engage in this act? If you are as wise as the Lord made you, then the answer is surely no! Please pray this prayer with me:

Most Gracious and Heavenly Father, I come to You with a humble heart and I ask You to forgive me for every sexual immoral sin that I have engaged in. I pray for freedom God, freedom from every chain that has been bound to me while I was committing these sinful acts. I pray for every stronghold to be

broken and every soul tie to be destroyed. Lord, I pray that You allow Your Holy Spirit to dwell within me. Help me to live for You in all I do, in Jesus name. Amen.

Chapter 26: Salvation Through Works

Raegina relied heavily on the fact that she had done so much for ministry. She thought that she had somehow "earned" her way into heaven because she sacrificed so much of her time towards the church and the spreading of the gospel. Let's take a look at her "good works":

- Her involvement with the evangelism team
- Her podcasts

- Being the daughter of a Pastor
- Her Facebook following
- Attending church regularly
- Teaching children
- Past actions that demonstrated love of God
- Leading some to Christ

In the world, we do in fact rely on our experience in whichever field we are in to qualify us for future positions. This is not so with the Kingdom of God. Rage was fooled by her own deeds being sufficient to pay the cost of her entrance into heaven. This is a problem with many believers. We disregard the "sin" in our life, and try to work our way into heaven. Or if we do sin, we simply state a "God forgive me" prayer without true repentance for the sins that we have committed. We have to make an about face from the sin, making a 180 degree turn from that sin and back to Christ. Ignoring, justifying or tolerating the presence of sin will have us in the same state that Rage found herself in. No amount of good deeds will suffice. If that was the true way into earning a place in heaven, then Jesus would not have had to die on the cross. Furthermore, if we in fact believe that getting to heaven is our primary reason for salvation, we have missed the sacrifice Jesus made entirely. We are reminded in Romans 8:38,

For I am persuaded that neither death nor life, nor angels nor principalities nor powers, nor things present nor things to come, nor height nor depth, nor any other created thing, shall be able to separate us from the love of God which is in Christ Jesus our Lord.

This verse shows us the depth of the love that God has for us. If someone loves you to the point of allowing their only child to die in place of you, how selfish would it be to ignore their love and just desire the benefits? His love cries out to the heart of believer in every way. We call women who want to be with a man based solely on the benefits of being with him (whether it involves financial increase, fame, or status) a gold digger. We know that there is rarely true love involved as that person would be out the door if anything happened that jeopardized the benefits. If you have been looking at salvation as your ticket into heaven, you should examine your heart. God is looking for true love, His bride, and not gold diggers who are after beneficial gains of being with Him. I may add that not only does He love us and desire us, but we NEED HIM. satan's job in the garden places us in a place where it is impossible to be without Jesus. We can't be reconciled. I remember when I worked so hard in the church, I am sure God was pleased, but even if I worked 1,000 years, it wouldn't be sufficient. The risk of sounding redundant overtakes me but I will repeat my former plea to tell you how little our righteousness is in God's eyes. Isaiah 64:6 states:

We are all infected and impure with sin. When we display our righteous deeds, they are nothing but filthy rags. Like autumn leaves, we wither and fall, and our sins sweep us away like the wind.

Can you imagine a rag full of filth like vomit, menstrual blood, feces and urine? This is what our righteous deeds are before God. They are insufficient. There is nothing that we can do in any way that eliminates the need of Jesus in our life, working and shaping us back into the image of God. We were indeed created in His image and His likeness, but sin has distorted us. Without the working of the Holy Spirit every day in our lives, we will never be in a place where we are prepared for eternity. Rage's belief in the fact that her "sacrifices" were enough were crumbled as she stood before a Holy God that is judging according to His Word. He is not judging how much better you are than Sister Sally. It doesn't matter how much more than everyone else you show up for prayer meetings. God looks at our hearts, motives, and our actions of relying on the work that is done on the cross. Beloved please do not fall into the deception of thinking that doing a work for the kingdom of God will be enough. Seek God, who leads us to walk in the Spirit of God. Pray and ask Him to give you the Holy Spirit, ask Him to help you to live according to His word. Lean on Him through faith to produce the good works that God is looking for in us. Don't rely on yourself, as you will be deceived as Rage was. Our works are not enough.

Chapter 27: Unforgiveness

Rage harbored unforgiveness towards her sister in her heart. This was evident in the fact that she did whatever she could to sabotage her sister in every way. She even went as far to have sex with her sister's boyfriends and eventually her fiancé to get back at her. Now in Rage's case, she resented her sister for being a true follower of Christ. Her sister was abstaining from sexually immoral acts and from the evidence produced in Christ's words to Raegina, He was with her sister. Perhaps her sister was mean spirited towards Raegina at one time or another. The story doesn't reveal, but for whichever reason, Rage's behavior was in some ways fueled by her sister's dedication to Christ. While many may sympathize with Raegina for being the "black sheep" of the family, there was no room for sympathy on judgment day for her because she refused to forgive.

Many of us have been wronged in one way or another. If you haven't beloved, keep living. At some time or another, someone somewhere will do something that violates you. We all have a choice on how we decide to handle that situation when it comes. Some of us decide to cut people off, never speaking to them again because they have done us wrong. (By some of us I mean myself if I am being honest), and that's not the way that the bible instructs us. The bible tells us that we should love them, in spite of the opposition. Let's look into the book of Matthew:

You have heard that it was said, 'You shall love your neighbor and hate your enemy.' But I say to you, love your enemies, bless those who curse you, do good to those who hate you, and pray for those who spitefully use you and persecute you, that you may be sons of your Father in heaven; for He makes His sun rise on the evil and on the good, and sends rain on the just and on the unjust. For if you love those who love you, what reward have you? Do not even the tax collectors do the same? And if you greet your brethren only, what do you do more than others? Do not even the tax collectors do so? Therefore you shall be perfect, just as your Father in heaven is perfect.

Now you may read this and say, "that is impossible to do." Indeed it can seem that way. To *actually bless* people who have wronged you and done evil towards you sounds insane! One may believe that you would have to be perfect to do that. This verse leaves no room for imperfection as Jesus Himself has made it clear that we are to "be ye perfect, as your father in heaven is perfect." We must continually go before God and ask Him to cleanse us from unforgiveness towards other people. I find myself remembering things people did to me years ago, and not wanting to even associate myself with them. I have to go to the Father and ask Him to heal my heart and my mind from keeping unforgiveness in my heart for them. I know it sounds unbelievable in this world that we live in. I want to ask you how badly do you want to live like Christ has instructed you? How much do you long for the righteousness of Christ to dwell in your heart? If you have the darkness of unforgiveness, there is no room for the Holy Spirit. Light will not commune with darkness. It took me a while to discover this truth. You get so caught up with feeling used, feeling unappreciated, feeling like someone violated you and they could be 100% wrong, but the Word of God, spoken by **Jesus Himself,** tells us to forgive. Maybe it will take writing the names of those who have wronged you down and including them in your prayers. Perhaps it will mean taking those same names and asking God to help you to forgive each person truly and fully. I remember I met someone and he was interested in winning my heart. He went and evaluated my every move and thought about what type of things he would have to do to be in my life. He thought maybe I would want him to pay for my hair to be styled, or maybe I would like for him to attend church services. He eventually told me that he made up in his mind that he would do "whatever it takes". This is the attitude we have to have in the arena of forgiveness. You may have very valid reasons for why you do not wish to forgive a person who has wronged you. You may know that this person means you no earthly (or heavenly for that matter) good. This doesn't change what has been instructed in God's Word. We simply must forgive.

What is the consequence if you don't forgive? Maybe even after hearing that entire plea for you to forgive others has not convinced you that you should forgive. I know that my examples are not as extreme as some people that have been molested, raped, mistreated, abused, put to shame, given away, abandoned or nearly killed. The Word of God gives no leeway. We still have to find it in our hearts to forgive. This is not a choice. Let's look back into the Word of God to see what in fact happens if you do not forgive:

Then Peter came to Him and said, "Lord, how often shall my brother sin against me, and I

forgive him? Up to seven times?" Jesus said to him, "I do not say to you, up to seven times, but up to seventy times seven. Therefore, the kingdom of heaven is like a certain king who wanted to settle accounts with his servants. And when he had begun to settle accounts, one was brought to him who owed him ten thousand talents. But as he was not able to pay, his master commanded that he be sold, with his wife and children and all that he had, and that payment be made. The servant therefore fell down before him, saying, 'Master, have patience with me, and I will pay you all.' Then the master of that servant was moved with compassion, released him, and forgave him the debt. "But that servant went out and found one of his fellow servants who owed him a hundred denarii; and he laid hands on him and took him by the throat, saying, 'Pay me what you owe!' So his fellow servant fell down at his feet and begged him, saying, 'Have patience with me, and I will pay you all.' And he would not, but went and threw him into prison till he should pay the debt. So when his fellow servants saw what had been done, they were very grieved, and came and told their master all that had been done. Then his master, after he had called him, said to him, 'You wicked servant! I forgave you all that debt because you begged me. Should you not also have had compassion on your fellow servant, just as I had pity on you?' And his master was angry, and delivered him to the torturers until he should pay all that was due to him. "So My heavenly Father also will do to you if each of you, from his heart, does not forgive his brother his trespasses."

This scripture makes up my mind to forgive, no matter what. This reveals that you have to forgive others or be in danger of the hellfire. Think about this for a moment. If someone who has wronged you has that type of power, the power to make you guilty of sin terrible enough to be punished in hell, do you leave it with them? I hope not. Beloved, nothing is worth your salvation! Nothing is worth pursuing that will place you outside of God's presence for eternity. Nothing. Let me continue to break down the significance of what it is this scripture is saying. This servant owed the master the equivalence of 200,000 years' worth of wages. The master forgave him and then he goes and finds someone who owed him a couple month's wages and try to punish him. The difference between the two numbers is staggering. This is the same way God's view on our forgiveness of the sins and transgressions of others. It is as simple. Matthew 6:14 states, ***if we do not forgive others, our heavenly Father will not forgive us.*** Can you imagine being held accountable for every sin that you have ever committed? Even if by some miracle you have only committed one sin one time, your repayment to God is more than you can ever handle. So we should willfully forgive so that we can in return be forgiven. Won't you cry out for freedom from unforgiveness today dear reader?

Chapter 28: Rage Was Unrepentant

Rage was in the church. She had many followers on social media. She was the daughter of a minister. Nevertheless, Rage still was indulgent in her sins of choice. Even up until the last moment she had on earth, she made a choice to keep loving the sin that she was in and felt that she "was living" when she indulged in her transgressions against God. I stress emphasis on the part of Rage's transgressions *against* God because that is what sin is aimed against, God's standards. Sadly, many people who identify as Christians make this a normal practice in their lives. They sin over and over again, never displaying the true heart of repentance when they ask for forgiveness. Imagine if you had someone who you are in a relationship with. They come to you and tell you that they have been cheating on you. You love this person and you want to make it work, so you forgive that person. Time passes and this person keeps making decisions that are hurting you. They say they are sorry, but their behavior doesn't change. Their attitude is that they are not perfect, and you shouldn't expect them to be. You try to explain over and over what your expectations are from them and plead with them to limit their infractions against your standards, but they don't listen. It's the same cycle day after day, month after month, year after year. Would you not come to the conclusion that everything that this person has done to you is something he/she doesn't care about? To me it would be extremely obvious through their actions. This is very much the same way we treat God when we are unrepentant. This is what we are doing when we keep that hidden or open sin in spite of God's word which forbids it. Every year, I see many people who practice the sin of homosexuality flaunting their sin in the street in parades all over the globe. They even express it as "pride". I don't understand how some of these very same people believe that God should just accept "who they are" and allow them to commit acts which God describes as an abomination to Him. Fornicators are the same. The are quick to judge those practicing homosexuality, when they are having babies out of wedlock. When you consider the book of 2 Chronicles 7:14,

Then if my people who are called by my name will humble themselves and pray and seek My face and turn from their wicked

ways, I will hear from heaven and will forgive their sins and restore their land.

This bible verse shows the true act of repentance. It involves humbling yourself. This is a far cry from the pride that is expressed by many about the acts they commit against God. Being humble means being able to accept the truth of God's Word and making sure that you are ready to do whatever it requires to please God. The second act of repentance is to pray. So many of us skip this vital step. Maybe this particular sin has control over you to the point where you can't fight it off. This is why you need to pray to the Master for help. There is not enough prayer in the churches, in the homes, in the life of believers. People are instead just wallowing in their situations, or complaining to other people about the pain and confusion sin causes in your life. When you are truly humble and you are ready to repent, you will cry out to God and trust that He will help you to turn away from your sins. Beloved, do not get entrapped in a sin and then bask in it through boasting about it. This is an act of mocking God, His Word and most of all His power. The next part of this scripture is to seek His face. This is something that a lot of people misconstrue. Instead of seeking God's face, they seek His hand in their life. They want God to bless them, bless their family, cause them to shine, make their enemies their footstool. All the while, they never really know who God really is. As a woman, I get upset when a man comes to me and he can't even look me in my eyes. It's upsetting when all he does is look at your body parts, probably imagining all the sinful acts he could commit with you. I have no respect and lose all interest when any man does this. How much more do you believe God feels this way? When we seek His hand, we are after His riches, His glory and His favor in our lives. We don't take the time to hear Him and seek His presence just to be close to Him. I don't 100% blame this on the believer as many churches invite people to Christ based only on His promises. Whether it be eternal life, prosperity, favor, or just a free "get out of hell free card" - people flock to the altar, anxious to receive their free gift from God. Only a few ever get to the point where they desire to know God personally. We as the church need to stress the importance of getting to know God for *yourself*. I thank God for sending me to a church that taught me that valuable lesson. Yes, the Pastor can pray, yes evangelists can spread the message of the gospel. However, we have a mandate on our life to place God first in our lives. Not His hand, but God Himself. Are you seeking His face today?

The last part of repentance is turning from our wicked ways. This is not the time to try to measure the severity of sin from one sin to another. Sin is sin. God wants us to turn from it. I have heard many people say, "Make a 360 degree turn." This is not truth. If you make a 360 degree turn, you have made a complete circle. This leads you back to the sin. We need to turn 180 degrees, which turns us away from the sin in question and into the opposite direction. So many of us are somewhere way before 180 degrees, perhaps at 90 degrees, where we turn from the sin but we are still not headed in the right direction. We have to conclude within ourselves that we do not want to do that which is evil in God's sight, claim the victory over it and continue in Christ Jesus. If we do not truly repent, then sin will be forever present in our life and we will always be in wrong standing with the Lord. Seek out a repentant heart and trust in God to carry you through.

When you have done all of these things, then you are ready to receive from God. More importantly, He is ready to hear your prayers. Notice in this scripture, all the actions we need to take are listed prior to stating that God will hear from heaven and heal our land. Now, our land is not necessarily the United States, or the Philippines. It is not your front yard or your workplace. Your land is your life, your being. God wants to heal **you** from whichever stronghold, illness, pain, and soul tie that is making your life hard and more importantly, separating you from God. He wants to deliver you. WE MUST KEEP THIS SCRIPTURE IN OUR HEARTS AND TRUST WHAT IT SAYS to be able to receive the things you need from God. It is so necessary. If you have to, please read this section of the book again. I really desire for this to be in your spirit.

Chapter 29: Rage Walked According to Her Flesh

Rage's life was driven by her own desires. This is why she was led to do so many things that are contrary to God's Word. When we come to Jesus Christ and accept Him as our Lord and Savior, then we must submit ourselves to Him in every way. If we do not, and continue to live life as we did before we received salvation, God is not able to operate in us fully. The Holy Spirit is our first eternal gift from God. When He is allowed to work in us, the righteousness of God produces good works inside of us. Unfortunately, the opposite is also true. In Rage's case, because she blatantly ignored the will of God for her life and went after her own sinful desires, the work that was produced in her life was evil.

Galations 5:16-21

I say then: Walk in the Spirit, and you shall not fulfill the lust of the flesh. For the flesh lusts against the Spirit, and the Spirit against the flesh; and these are contrary to *one another, so that you do not do the things that you wish. But if you are led by the Spirit, you are not under the law. Now the works of the flesh are evident, which are: adultery, fornication, uncleanness, lewdness, idolatry, sorcery, hatred, contentions, jealousies, outbursts of wrath, selfish ambitions, dissensions, heresies, envy, murders, drunkenness, revelries, and the like; of which I tell you beforehand, <u>just as I also told you in time past, that those who practice such things will not inherit the kingdom of God.</u>*

Paul is speaking to the Galatians in this text, but we are the current church. When we walk in the flesh and pursue the desires of our own heart, certain things are produced. If you look into the passage above, many of these fruits were present in her life. Let's look at a list of them:

- ***Envy*** - she envied her sister.
- ***Drunkenness*** was another-as she was completely inebriated at the club.
- She also displayed ***fornication*** – obviously, while sleeping with Omere.
- She had ***lewdness*** - in the way she was dressed for the club.

- She also had **hatred** for her sister
- **Contentions** in regards to her sister
- She also had *jealousy* towards her sister.
- She openly displayed **outbursts of wrath** with Omere
- More than anything, she had **selfish ambitions** in all her pursuits
- **Dissensions** - her life revolved around it.
- **Revelries** were a part of her life displayed in her clubbing and behavior after the club.

In looking over my life, I remember when I walked after the flesh. No one ever told me: or should I say, I never took the time to see what type of fruit my life was producing. It just made perfect sense that if I went to church and read my bible occasionally, I would be among those in heaven and in good standing with God. All of the bad fruit was simply a part of everyday life for me. The saddest part of it all is that I was claiming Christianity despite the production of the bad fruit in my life. Maybe you see some of these fruit in your life or in those around you. I encourage you to step out of the flesh. Get into a life of prayer, commit your every thought and conversation to the Lord. Get into His presence through worship and openness with God. Lean on Him when hard times come, and when you are tempted to resort back to those things of the flesh.

This scripture emphasizes that those who do such things will NOT INHERIT the kingdom of God. I remember having a vision of myself in the restroom, looking at the mirror. I said out loud, "I am so glad that I don't have to wear THAT anymore." I looked over and on a shelf in the bathroom was literally my flesh, it was as if my skin was a bodysuit and I had stepped out of it. We need to step out of our flesh and live for God. There are many people who are in churches, masquerading as children of the Most High, but the fruit they produce in their life is much different. Matthew 7:15-20 describes this to us.

"Beware of false prophets who come disguised as harmless sheep but are really vicious wolves. You can identify them by their fruit, that is, by the way they act. Can you pick grapes from thorn bushes, or figs from thistles? A good tree produces good fruit, and a bad tree produces bad fruit. A good tree can't produce bad fruit, and a bad tree can't produce good fruit. So every tree that does not produce good fruit is chopped down and thrown into the fire. Yes, just as you can identify a tree by its fruit, so you can identify people by their actions.

This scripture shows us the truth behind people and their relationship with Christ. If you see people producing the bad fruit, something in their life is not right. Maybe they haven't been performing the self-evaluations that are needed in order to make sure that they are in right standing with God. Perhaps, they have not learned that they should not walk in the flesh. It is something that you don't hear preached every day but it is vitally important. Paul is saying that you can be thrown into the fire when you produce the wrong fruit. This is definitely something for us to be careful about. Here are a few pointers:

1. **Check your thought patterns**: thoughts are the spirit form of actions. Most of the sins that we commit are ones that we have mapped out in our head prior to the actual action that produced the sin. Change your stinking thinking patterns and put on the mind of Christ through meditation on His Word, prayer and confession to God about your evil thoughts and desires.

2. **Surround yourself with people who are going to cultivate the gifting of God in you.** Evaluate your friendships. Though we may love and respect our friends (many of them have been around for many years), we have to be mindful that evil communication corrupts good character. When we allow people who are not led by the Spirit of God in our lives, they can influence us negatively. The bible

commands us to be separate from them. I have lost many friends because God knew their ways would eventually pull me away from Him. Are you willing to be separate from your friends for God?

3. **Pray, praise, and worship**- The more you draw closer to God, the more He will draw closer to you. You are as close to God as you desire to be. If He seems distant, reevaluate your time schedule and make more time for Him. We just have to make the first step in the right direction and He is faithful to show up and change our entire lives.

4. **Reach out**- Isolation is not good when you are part of the Body of Christ. If your ear decided "I want to hear on my own, not on the side of the head," and then jumped off and landed, it wouldn't be long before it withered and decomposed. The same goes for you, when you make it a habit to separate from the people of God. You will not be able to grow and flourish the way that God designed us all to.

There are some people who do indeed walk in the Spirit. These people's lives are led by the Spirit of God. They do self-examinations. The will of God is what they seek after, and therefore, their life looks very different from those who are walking in the flesh. This is because when you walk in the Spirit, the fruit that your life will produce is much different from those who are walking in the flesh. Let's look into our Word to find out what it says about walking in the Spirit.

But the Holy Spirit produces this kind of fruit in our lives: love, joy, peace, patience, kindness, goodness, faithfulness, gentleness, and self-control. There is no law against these things! Those who belong to Christ Jesus have nailed the passions and desires of their sinful nature to his cross and crucified them there. Since we are living by the Spirit, let us follow the Spirit's leading in every part of our lives. Let us not become conceited, or provoke one another, or be jealous of one another.

You see a vast difference between those who walk in the spirit and those who walk in the flesh. They do things differently; their life is different. They are able to produce great fruit that benefits themselves and others in a positive manner. One very important portion of the passage says that they have nailed their passions and desires of their sinful nature to the cross. Can you honestly say that you have nailed your passions to the cross? Are you only motivated to do the things of God's heart? Be honest in your answer. I know that we live in a society that has made it normalcy to hide your truth and live behind images that are simply made up. This will not work in the Kingdom of God. The bible tells us how to identify the fruit that our life is producing and to be able to judge our spiritual life by it. If you are producing bad fruit, it is time for you to repent and get it right with the Lord. If you are hanging around those who are producing bad fruit, it is time to separate yourselves from them. Beloved, please do not wait until it is too late.

My final plea to you...

In understanding all that God has given me to write to you, I pray that you are able to understand the urgency of the matter. We don't know the day, nor the hour when Christ is to return. Therefore, it is imperative that we live each moment as if it is our last. For those of you that are yet struggling to find a starting point right now, I will tell you to seek His face. Make God your number one priority, and pleasing Him your number one goal. Make time for Him in the morning, read your word whenever you get a chance, as often as possible. Pray all the time. Pray while you're cooking, pray while you're showering, driving, and even combing your hair. The beauty of prayer is that it doesn't have to be formal in any way. It is just a conversation with God. Tell Him your thoughts, your fears, your desires to live for Him. Maybe you are unsure of who He is or even if all that has been told to you about Him is even true. Tell Him that too. Some of the most beautiful testimonies I have ever heard have come from people who simply told God "If you are real, show me." If your heart is earnestly seeking Him, you will find Him. Remember what the Bible tells us:

Isaiah 55:6-7

Seek the LORD while He may be found; call upon Him while He is near. Let the wicked forsake his way and the unrighteous man his thoughts; and let him return to the LORD, and He will have compassion on him, and to our God, for He will abundantly pardon.

I believe that if we are seeking God truly with our whole heart, this verse will become the testimony of our lives. God desires a relationship, a true relationship with each and every one of us. He longs for us to turn away from sin and to be reconciled to Him through Jesus Christ. All it takes is having a made up mind that is ready to serve Him no matter what it takes. The verse above petitions the unrighteous and the wicked to forsake his way and to seek God. It promises compassion from God towards that person. His mercy is renewed every morning and there is nothing that you have done that makes you invalid for the Kingdom of God. If your heart is yearning, in the way that I know it is, start right now today in your journey back into the heart of God. No matter what it is that you are going through, no matter what sins you have been guilty of, God is faithful and He is able. I am convinced God is calling you to Him even right now. Many of you have been hurt in your life. You may have had many things happen to you that have caused you to make questionable decisions. Do not be discouraged or fearful in coming to God. He is able to heal even your deepest wounds. In parting, I want to give you the words of Peter, which have comforted me during my toughest trials:

1 Peter 5:10

And the God of all grace, who called you to his eternal glory in Christ, after you have suffered a little while, will Himself restore you and make you strong, firm and steadfast.

But what if I don't Believe??

Questions I have heard that you may have about faith....

I don't believe in Hell

I have heard this many times. There are people who are open to believing God and everything in His Word, aside from eternal damnation. Undoubtedly each person may have various reasons for not believing this, all of them reasonable to some extent. What I want my readers and audience to understand is that in the depiction of Rage's life as well as my own, it is a very real place. I personally pray that those who are fooled into believing any different will take a hard look at the truths that are revealed in God's Words numerous times over. Jesus spoke on it

Himself. Nevertheless people seem to have looked over that truth and want to brush it away as "parables". Let's take a little time to explore the reasoning behind some belief systems on hell...

He is a loving God. Why would He send anyone to such a horrible place?

God is indeed a loving God. So loving that He willingly gave His own Son for our sins. He loves us so much that He has given us time to get our hearts in line with His Word. He has sent His Holy Spirit to cleanse us, pray for us and live in us, causing us to live for Him if we so choose. He has sent preachers, teachers, prophets and His Word the Bible, to warn us about what is to come if we do not get our hearts in line with what He is saying. Nonetheless, the Bible reveals to us that the day will come that He will judge the earth. Here are some Bible verses that reveal the truth of judgment and punishment for those who are found lacking.

Isaiah 13:11
Thus I will punish the world for its evil and the wicked for their iniquity; I will also put an end to the arrogance of the proud And abase the haughtiness of the ruthless.

Zephaniah 1:12

"It will come about at that time That I will search Jerusalem with lamps, And I will punish the men who are stagnant in spirit, who say in their hearts, 'The LORD will not do good or evil!'

Hebrews 9:27
And inasmuch as it is appointed for men to die once and after this comes judgment.

Jeremiah 21:14
"But I will punish you according to the results of your deeds," declares the LORD, "And I will kindle a fire in its forest that it may devour all its environs."

Romans 2: 5-6
*But because of your stubbornness and unrepentant heart you are storing up wrath for yourself in the day of wrath and revelation of the righteous judgment of God, who **WILL RENDER TO EACH PERSON ACCORDING TO HIS DEEDS.***

Beloved, if you truly cannot see the truth about judgment day and what is to come, I pray that you will seek God for yourself. I dare you to ask God, "What is the truth?" I encourage you to truly wait and expect an answer. Each day until God has revealed this to you, keep an open heart and mind to receive it. I know that God will show you, either through another conversation, a dream or vision, or just an inward knowing that all that I say to you, all that the bible has said to you is truth.

We won't be judged on things we say or on the things we post on social media...

In the story of Rage, we saw that she was judged even down to what she posted on social media. I can understand why so many people would see error in this. Being that I am such an avid social media user, I know that many look at it as just a fun way to pass time. Many are careless in what they post and how it makes them or others look due to this fact. People sometimes do this because they feel other people are using social media the same way. I have heard comments like, "it's just social media. Why are people taking it so seriously?" In my own personal experience, there are so many people who take everything posted serious. I have posted bible verses and had people flood my inboxes with questions and confessions about what they are doing wrong in their life. I have had times when I spent hours praying with people about even Rage's story, as it touched their hearts and minds in such a way that they wanted to be prepared for judgment. Even my own

Facebook following started because of a post I made years ago, that turned people's hearts (both good and bad) about eternity. Many times, people have remembered something I posted and told me much later how it helped them in some way shape or form. One can only assume that as much as the positive posts I have placed on my Facebook have helped others, my more negative ones have hurt others. If you think about the fact that your words will definitely be judged, it's only logical to say even the written ones count. Here are a few Bible verses to help you to better understand.

Matthew 12:36-37
"But I tell you that every careless word that people speak, they shall give an accounting for it in the Day of Judgment. "For by your words you will be justified, and by your words you will be condemned."

Romans 14:12-13
Yes, each of us will give a personal account to God. So let's stop condemning each other. Decide instead to live in such a way that you will not cause another believer to stumble and fall.

Romans 14:21

It is better not to eat meat or drink wine or do anything else if it might cause another believer to stumble.

2 Peter 2:1-2

But there were also false prophets in Israel, just as there will be false teachers among you. They will cleverly teach destructive heresies and even deny the Master who bought them. In this way, they will bring sudden destruction on themselves. Many will follow their evil teaching and shameful immorality. And because of these teachers, the way of truth will be slandered.

I personally came to the conclusion that whatever I posted on social media would be pleasing to God. In reading these bible verses as I write this book, I have realized that it was God that led me to do decide this. The result is that thousands of people from places all over the world like Guyana, Pakistan, Australia, the Philippines, South Africa, and many countries I have never even heard of have been changed and encouraged. I have prayer partners in Trinidad, sisters in Christ that are in France, and people everywhere who are affected everyday by what I post from my own phone. Beloved, don't you see the power in surrendering everything, even your social media to God for His use? How many lives could you change?

Hell is here on earth. Everyday I see people suffering...

The truth is that if you watch the news, you will hear so many troubling stories of tragedies taking place in this world. People are committing senseless acts of murder, rape, and kidnapping. There is a whole industry based on selling people as slaves of sex. Even parents are killing children and vice versa. No wonder so many people believe the hell on earth theory. How can there exist a place more evil than the one that we live in where people die everyday from diverse diseases, and there are so many deaths from natural disasters and murders that go unsolved. Dear reader, the present day evil is enough to drive anyone to the question of why and how a good God that loves us so much would allow so many tragedies. I could try to sum it up in a quick paragraph or even an entire book. Nonetheless, the fact remains that evil is present on this earth. Yet and still, there is far more evil that awaits those that are not properly prepared for eternity.

The Horrors of Hell

I find it strange that so many people are able to view heaven as a real place, yet are quick to dispute hell. Many believe that there will be streets paved in gold, no more sadness, no more pain, and no more death. The fact that we know heaven as a place where pain cannot exist lets us know that we will be able to feel in eternity. That can be a good and bad thing. When we are talking about hell, there are truths that are unimaginable. Many of them are those that were spoken by Jesus Himself. However, even some of the Old Testament books tell us about a hell that exists and even go into grave detail of what we can expect. Let's take a look at some of them now.

Matthew 13:40-42

"Just as the weeds are sorted out and burned in the fire, so it will be at the end of the world. The Son of Man will send his angels, and they will remove from his Kingdom everything that causes sin and all who do evil. <u>And the angels will throw them</u>

into the fiery furnace, where there will be weeping and gnashing of teeth.

2 Peter 2:4
For God did not spare even the angels who sinned. He threw them into hell, in gloomy pits of darkness, where they are being held until the Day of Judgment.

Revelation 20:10
Then the devil, who had deceived them, was thrown into the fiery lake of burning sulfur, joining the beast and the false prophet. There they will be tormented day and night forever and ever.

Revelation 20:14-15

Then death and the grave were thrown into the lake of fire. This lake of fire is the second death. And anyone whose name was not found recorded in the Book of Life was thrown into the lake of fire.

Jude 1:7
And don't forget Sodom and Gomorrah and their neighboring towns, which were filled with immorality and every kind of

sexual perversion. <u>Those cities were destroyed by fire and serve as a warning of the eternal fire of God's judgment.</u>

Revelation 21:8
But cowards, unbelievers, the corrupt, murderers, the immoral, those who practice witchcraft, idol worshipers, and all liars—<u>their fate is in the fiery lake of burning sulfur. This is the second death.</u>

Mark 9:47
And if your eye causes you to sin, gouge it out. It's better to enter the Kingdom of God with only one eye than to have two eyes and be <u>thrown into hell, 'where the maggots never die and the fire never goes out.'</u>

Beloved, even if you only approach God for clarification on the truths of hell, I believe that it will lead your heart to desire a relationship with the Father in Heaven. There are many who ask how can a loving God prepare such an evil place, It was prepared for satan and his angels. However, because satan has enticed the hearts of man going way back to Eve in the garden, there are people who have chosen the path satan paved instead of God's path and have not been able to make it to the eternal abode that has been prepared for them. The bible tells us that hell has enlarged herself. I pray that there is found no room made for any of you.

References

- Scripture quotations are taken from the Holy Bible, New Living Translation, copyright ©1996, 2004, 2007, 2013, 2015 by Tyndale House Foundation. Used by permission of Tyndale House Publishers, Inc., Carol Stream, Illinois 60188. All rights reserved.

- NIV references- The Holy Bible: New International Version. Grand Rapids, MI: Zondervan, 2011.

- AMP references- The Holy Bible: Amplified Version. Grand Rapids, MI: Zondervan Publishing House, 1987. Print.

- NKJV references-Scripture taken from the New King James Version®. Copyright © 1982 by Thomas Nelson. Used by permission. All rights reserved.

- Slick, Matt. "What are the the verses that mention hell in the new testament?" *Christian*

Apologetics and Research Ministry. (n.d.), from https://carm.org/what-are-the-verses-that-mention-hell

- Forkner, Doug. (2016). In the twinkling of an eye. Retrieved from http://timothybibleclass.org/thoughts-from-timothy/in-the-twinkling-of-an-eye/

- "Christian." Merriam-Webster.com. Merriam-Webster, n.d. Web. 17 June 2017.

- "Grace." Merriam-Webster.com. Merriam-Webster, n.d. Web. 17 June 2017

- Detestable. (n.d.). Retrieved June 17, 2017, from https://www.merriam-webster.com/dictionary/detestable

- Synonyms for "detestable" Oxford University Press. *The Oxford American College Dictionary.* Published G.P. Putnam's Sons, 2002
- Dominic Bryan (2000). *Orange Parades: The Politics of Ritual, Tradition and Control.* Pluto Press.

- "Salvation." Merriam-Webster.com. Merriam-Webster, n.d. Web. 17 June 2017

- Saint Augustine. (n.d.). BrainyQuote.com. Retrieved June 17, 2017, from BrainyQuote.com Web site: https://www.brainyquote.com/quotes/quotes/s/saintaugus148529.html

- "authority"Oxford University Press. *The Oxford American College Dictionary*. Published G.P. Putnam's Sons, 2002

- "influence" Oxford University Press. *The Oxford American College Dictionary*. Published G.P. Putnam's Sons, 2002

- "master" Oxford University Press. *The Oxford American College Dictionary*. Published G.P. Putnam's Sons, 2002

- "ruler" Oxford University Press. *The Oxford American College Dictionary*. Published G.P. Putnam's Sons, 2002

- "power"-Oxford University Press. *The Oxford American College Dictionary*. Published G.P. Putnam's Sons, 2002

- "remission"-Oxford University Press. *The Oxford American College Dictionary.* Published G.P. Putnam's Sons, 2002

- "Lord"-Oxford University Press. *The Oxford American College Dictionary.* Published G.P. Putnam's Sons, 2002

God .Rage. Eternity Study Guide

Coming soon! God .Rage. Eternity study guide!

- Gives deeper insight into the book chapter by chapter
- Perfect for use in Bible Study Groups and school settings
- Helps readers to gain a more personal insight on what God is doing in his/her life.
- Includes a notes section for adding bible verses!!

www.Iamstephanietramaine.com